# Emigrants and Expats

# Emigrants and Expats

A guide to sources on UK emigration
and residents overseas

Roger Kershaw

PUBLIC RECORD OFFICE

Public Record Office Readers' Guide No. 20

Public Record Office
Richmond
Surrey TW9 4DU

www.pro.gov.uk/

ISBN 1 903365 32 5

A catalogue record for this book is available from the British Library

Front cover photographs: Personal history card of Richard Browne, child emigrant to
New Zealand, 1940–41 (DO 131/15); Carrying of Childen's Overseas Reception Board
(CORB) child evacuees to New Zealand, 1940–41 (DO 131/15)

Printed by The Cromwell Press Ltd, Trowbridge, Wiltshire

# Contents

# Illustrations

# Acknowledgements

The author would like to thank the following colleagues in the PRO for their kind assistance in the production of this Guide: Hugh Alexander, Dr Amanda Bevan, John Carr, Dr Paul Carter, Jane Crompton, James Cronan, Bruno Derrick, Guy Grannum, Anne Kilminster, Sheila Knight, Sarah Leach, Ann Morton, Kathryn Sleight, William Spencer, Graham Stanley and John Wood. Special reference should be made to Stella Colwell and Hilary Jones who helped me tremendously with the research into this subject.

I would also like to thank Adrian Allan, Archivist of the University of Liverpool Library; Melanie Barber, Deputy Librarian and Archivist of the Lambeth Palace Library; Debbie Beavis, DataMarine; Else Churchill, Genealogy Officer, Society of Genealogists; Dawn Littler, Curator of the Merseyside Maritime Museum Archive and Library; Clive Luckman, Genealogical Society of Victoria, Australia; Paul Milner, Federation of Genealogical Societies, USA; and Connie Potter, Family History Specialist, National Archives and Records Administrator, USA.

# Preface

People emigrate for many reasons. Sometimes the decision is a voluntary one. At other times it has been forced upon people. Reasons to emigrate voluntarily have included the need to seek religious or political freedom or the need to escape war or poverty. They can also include ambition and a desire to better oneself and grasp the opportunities available overseas. Enforced emigration relates mainly to transportation: a period of exile overseas in a British territory during which a convict would be forced to work productively and learn new habits of industry while at the same time benefit the development of the colonial economy.

Since the seventeenth century it has been estimated that Great Britain and Ireland have sent well over 10 million emigrants to the USA alone, along with 4 million to Canada and 1.5 million to Australasia. In total, more than 17 million persons have emigrated from the British Isles. As well as sending British citizens, the United Kingdom has acted as a transit centre for migrating Europeans, particularly Scandanavians, Dutch, German, Polish and Russian migrants who from about 1850 chose to emigrate to North America by travelling to Hull and then to Liverpool by train, prior to sailing out to the USA or Canada.

The Public Record Office (PRO) has many records relating to emigration but, because of the nature and limited scope of them, there can be no certainty of finding information on any particular individual. Involuntary emigrants such as those who were transported are easier to find than voluntary emigrants.

At present no institution in the UK is dedicated to the study of emigration in all its aspects. The PRO holds central government sources but millions of people emigrated through voluntary organizations and much information can still be found in the archives of the destination or recipient countries. The Merseyside Maritime Museum's Maritime Archive and Library, Albert Dock, Liverpool L3 4AQ, comes nearest to an emigration institution in the UK. The Library has a large selection of emigration literature including bibliographies and published passenger lists, finding aids to Australasian and North American emigration archives, and information sheets. It has also accessioned original emigrant letters, diaries and other material, and employs specialists in emigrant studies. On site as part of the Merseyside Museum and Galleries is an impressive Emigration exhibition the centrepiece of which is a reconstruction (dated 1851) of the steerage compartment (where emigrants normally travelled) of the *Shackamaxon*, a passenger liner. Another excellent source for emigration material is the Society of Genealogists, 14 Charterhouse Buildings, Goswell Road, London EC1M 7BA. The Society exists to promote the study of family history and is open to all. It has a large selection of books, articles, periodicals, microfilm, microfiche and CD-ROMS relating to the study of migration and these include lists of emigrants to Canada, 1749–1850, and lists of persons whose passage to Australia was assisted, 1828–96, together with numerous works relating to transportation and child migration.

It is important to note that most records relating to emigrants and expatriates overseas can be found in the archives of the receiving countries. Also, many British colonies changed hands through invasion and war and such records may also survive in other European archives, e.g. British Guiana was originally Dutch; Jamaica was Spanish; Tobago was German, then British, then French and then British again!

Whilst the PRO is a good source for Board of Trade passenger lists from 1890, few listings of emigrants can be found before this time. Much work has been done to publish those records that survive from original emigration sources in the UK together with those incoming lists compiled in the destination countries and many of these sources can be found in the PRO Library. Research has shown that the British government has always been more concerned with compiling records and data relating to immigrants rather than to emigrants, although published Parliamentary papers (also available at the PRO) do provide useful statistical information with regards to the subject.

As well as information relating to the physical departure of emigrants, there are many sources available concerning births, marriages and deaths of Britons overseas as civil registration records were kept abroad by British consulates or colonial authorities, and at sea by the masters of British merchant ships. The Family Records Centre (FRC) is the best place to consult such records, though copies of the indexes to most of these records are kept at the PRO. Others relating to religious registration housed at the Guildhall Library are explored within this guide and these provide a useful insight into how successful the life of an emigrant could be.

Probably the best central sources in terms of providing genealogical information are those relating to the transportation of criminals to North America (from 1615 to 1776) and to Australia (1787–1857). Again many of the sources have been published and are available in the PRO library but original sources can include transportation registers, which can lead researchers back to the formal court records.

For social and economic historians, PRO papers relating to the various and varied government assisted schemes to encourage emigration can provide fascinating reading. The schemes range from those fostering emigrants to flee the hardships of poverty and unemployment (such as the Irish potato famine in the mid-nineteenth century) to those assisting children to evacuate overseas during the Second World War (most notably the Children's Overseas Reception Board). Such records cut across government departments and pinpoint useful sources among Dominion Office papers, Poor Law records and the Ministry of Health, to name but three.

Valuable as they are, these varied central government records do not provide a full history of emigration and all its consequences. The printed annual lists of civil servants posted overseas such as the *Foreign Office Lists, Colonial Office Lists, Diplomatic Service Lists* and *Commonwealth Relations Office Lists* only record senior officials with brief biographical information. Historians therefore need to search in other archives and libraries (such as the Merseyside Maritime Museum and at the Society of Genealogists) for more information and that obligation is recognized in this guide. There are private papers to be researched. The autobiographies of people who left Britain to begin new lives overseas, whether temporarily or permanently, also call for consideration. Sometimes these reflections have derived from the great and the good but in other instances people who lived out of the public limelight have left reminiscences. Newspapers, of both the popular and quality kind, both within and outside the UK, constitute another valuable resource. The *Illustrated London News* for example (available at the PRO under reference ZPER 34) provides some wonderful illustrations of emigration.

# Introduction

The purpose of this readers' guide is to help researchers appreciate and understand the wide variety of records concerning emigrants held at the Public Record Office and at other archives. Its intended audience includes the genealogist seeking information relating to his or her own ancestry, as well as the social and economic historian interested in the history of emigration and its impact on British society over the past 400 years.

The guide aims to describe major waves of emigration and government-approved schemes as well as explaining clearly reasons for such movements and how patterns have changed over time. It discusses in depth those government departments responsible for overseeing emigration schemes and why certain records were preserved as archives and others were not. Above all, it offers guidance to what the records contain and some suggestions on how they might be used.

The structure of the guide allows the user to concentrate on specific key emigration sources, such as those records associated with the physical departure of emigrants (Chapter 1), and those relating to British people once they have settled in their new overseas destination (Chapter 5). A more detailed index at the back of the book allows the researcher to dip into the guide at his or her leisure.

The Public Record Office (PRO) at Kew, in south-west London, houses one of the finest, most complete archives in the world, running from the Domesday Book in 1086 to the present century. It holds the records for the central government of the United Kingdom (primarily of England and Wales, as Scotland and Northern Ireland have their own central record offices), as well the records of the law courts of England. In addition, it is also a major international archive, because of its vast holdings on the former British colonies, and on foreign relations over eight centuries.

Public records are not normally made available for reading until 30 years after the date of their final creation; thus a file opened in 1961 and closed in 1971 became available in 2002. Exceptions to this rule are noted in the text. Many documents which refer to individuals have much longer closure periods, to safeguard personal confidentiality; an obvious example is the census, which is closed for 100 years.

Records were produced in the course of government and the dispensing of justice. Many people now use them for the wholly different purpose of historical research.

Whether your field is family history or economic history, gender history or the history of crime, remember that the people who wrote down these records did so because there was an administrative need to do so. As a result, to find the answers we want, we often have to know something of how government and the courts operated, in order better to understand the surviving information.

The PRO bookshop, which runs a mail order service, currently holds about 250 family history titles: for more information write to the bookshop or check the PRO web site. The bibliographies in this book contain, besides works for further reading, information on various aids to finding and understanding records. Many of the books cited are available in the PRO, either in the Library, the Research Enquiries Room, or the reading rooms. Some can be bought in the shops at Kew and at the Family Records Centre (FRC). Most can be read in good reference libraries. If it is more convenient, you could try inter-library loan, through your local lending library.

The staff at the PRO and the FRC can help you with advice and guidance, but we can not actually do research for the public. The PRO and the FRC are open reference institutions, where readers have to come to the search rooms to conduct their own research. If this is not possible, then we can supply lists of professional researchers or record agents, who will undertake research for a fee. The arrangement between you and the agent will be of a purely private nature and the PRO and FRC can accept no responsibility for any aspect of the arrangements made between record agents and their clients.

The PRO has a very popular web site, at www.pro.gov.uk/ where you will find the latest information about the PRO's holdings, opening times, new accessions, publications, bookshop, etc., as well as the current e-mail address. It also contains copies of information leaflets which are sometimes more detailed in their instructions than the information given in this book. They are designed to be used in the reading rooms, and can be picked up when you arrive, or printed off the web site. The web site also provides access to our catalogue on computer.

The reading rooms at Kew are open to the public until 5 p.m., Monday to Saturday, with late night opening on Tuesday and Thursday until 7 p.m. They open at 9 a.m. except on Tuesdays (10 a.m.) and Saturdays (9.30 a.m.) Documents cannot be ordered until 9.30 a.m. Kew is closed on Sundays, public holidays and during stocktaking (one week, normally in December). There is a restaurant on site, where you can also eat your own food, and a shop.

Visitors to the PRO can now visit an exhibition featuring many of this nation's most famous documents. The exhibition, housed in the Education and Visitors' Centre (EVC) covers over 1,000 years of history and explores themes such as Crime and Punishment, Famous Names and War and Defence. Drawn from the National

Archive, the items on display illustrate many of the momentous events and famous characters that have shaped our history. The EVC is complemented by a programme of special events and exhibitions which aim to bring our collections to as wide an audience as possible. The items on display change at regular intervals. The centre is open during normal office hours. Last admissions are 15 minutes before closing.

You will need to obtain a reader's ticket at the PRO at Kew in order to see original records. This will be issued at Reception when you arrive, on production of some positive means of identification such as a passport, banker's card, or driving licence or, for foreign nationals, a passport or some other form of national identification document. Children aged 14 and over can be issued with a reader's ticket if they are either accompanied and vouched for by their parents (who have been able to produce their own identification to get a reader's ticket), or if they come with a letter of recommendation from their school, on headed notepaper and signed by the head teacher.

As part of the registration process, new readers are required to attend a 20-minute orientation tour to help them understand how to get the best out of the PRO's catalogues, copying services, and self-service open access systems. It also gives them the opportunity to learn how best to handle original records so that they can be used by future generations. Resources permitting, the PRO endeavours to run tours every 20 minutes until 2.40 p.m., Monday to Friday and throughout the morning on Saturdays. Please ensure you allow time for this when you plan your visit to the Office.

Large bags and coats are not allowed in the research areas at Kew. Lockable hangers are provided for coats, and there are lockers for other belongings. These take a £1 coin, which is returned after use. Pens and coloured pencils are not allowed in the reading rooms, but graphite pencils and laptop computers are (power points are available). Supplies of paper, tracing paper and pencils can be bought in the shops, which also sell magnifying sheets. If you want to trace anything, ask in the Reading Rooms for an acetate sheet to put over the document first. To help preserve the documents, please make use of the foam wedges and covered weights which are supplied (instructions for their use are on display).

The PRO welcomes readers with disabilities. There is a lift to all floors, and the facilities are wheelchair friendly. We have aids to help readers with impaired vision, but the totally blind are advised to come with a sighted friend. Equally, if you have mobility difficulties, it may be a good idea to come with a friend, as the PRO is a very large building, and there can be considerable distances to cover between different sources of information. If you contact us in advance, we can provide wheelchair assistance for the distance of more than 100 metres plus from the car park. You can look at our leaflet on *Physical Access to the Public Record Office and its Services* on our web site, or you can contact the PRO to ask for a copy to be sent to you.

The PRO's address and other details are:

| | |
|---|---|
| Post | Public Record Office, Kew, Richmond, Surrey TW9 4DU |
| Telephone | 020 8392 5200 |
| E-mail | enquiry@pro.gov.uk |
| Web site | www.pro.gov.uk/ |
| Fax | 020 8878 8905 |
| Minicom | 020 8392 9198 |

The FRC is open from 10 a.m. on Tuesdays, 9.30 a.m. on Saturdays, and 9 a.m. on the other weekdays. It closes at 7 p.m. on Tuesday and Thursday, and 5 p.m. on the other days. The FRC is closed on Sundays and public holidays with no closure period for stocktaking. A reader's ticket is not needed. Pens can be used, and there are power points for laptops in the PRO search room. There is a shop and an eating area in the building, and several places sell meals and sandwiches nearby. There are lockers if you wish to use them; a £1 coin is needed, but is returned after use.

The FRC has ramp access for wheelchairs and a lift to both floors. It also has three parking spaces reserved for disabled readers, which you have to book in advance by ringing 020 7533 6436. There are some motorized microfilm readers with zoom facilities, for disabled readers, and magnifiers are available for printed sources or copies. If you are totally blind or have limited mobility, try to come with a sighted or more mobile friend.

The Family Records Centre's address and other details are:

| | |
|---|---|
| Post | Family Records Centre, 1 Myddelton Street, London EC1R 1UW |
| Telephone | 020 8392 5300 – census enquiries |
| | 0870 243 7788 – birth, death and marriage certificate enquiries |
| Website | PRO web site at www.pro.gov.uk/ |
| | ONS web site at www.statistics.gov.uk/ |
| Fax | 020 8392 5307 |
| Minicom | 020 8392 5308 |

The ONS has a popular web site at www.statistics.gov.uk where you can look for information about ordering certificates, as well as finding out about new services.

An archive, such as the PRO, does not arrange its holdings by subject, but by the original institutional author – the supposed creator of the records. This means that to really get the best out of the sources, you have to have some idea of how the government and courts worked, who was responsible for what kinds of affairs, who is likely to have written to whom, what kind of information might have been collected or retained.

Records in the Public Record Office are divided into 'series', reflecting as far as possible what they were created for, and how they were used at the time. Each series has its own name and code, and each consists of individual 'pieces', which is what you order to be produced from the storage areas, or what you get yourself from a microfilm or microfiche cabinet. Each piece has a unique reference. This is made up of a department, a series number, and a piece number.

| | | |
|---|---|---|
| Department | e.g. HO | Home Office |
| + series number | e.g. HO 45 | Home Office: Registered Papers |
| + piece number | e.g. HO 45/2669 | EMIGRATION: Suggested depot for emigrants |

These references can be discovered from the various finding aids in the Public Record Office and via the web using our on-line catalogue.

The *PRO Guide* gives an overview of the history and content of all the records in the care of the PRO. Several printed copies are available, so you can sit and browse at leisure. Copies can also be seen at the FRC (PRO).

The *Guide* occupies several loose-leaf volumes, and is divided into three parts. Part 1 contains the history of government. Part 2 contains series descriptions in alphabetical order of series code for each series. Part 3 is the index to the other two parts. The main kinds of finding aid, hierarchically, below the *Guide*, are:

| | |
|---|---|
| *List* | A list of the pieces comprising a series of records, with dates and simple descriptions (a *descriptive list*: gives fuller indications of the contents of each document).<br><br>Lists in the Standard Set of series lists are filed in A4 binders, in alpha-numerical order of department/series number: there are several (colour-coded) sets of the full sequence from A to ZSPC – you are welcome to browse among them, but only the dark green paper set in the Research Enquiries Room is regularly updated.<br><br>Other lists will be found in the Non-Standard Sets, in the Research Enquiries Room and the Map and Large Document Room. These are often original or older finding aids, or published works. They each bear a small label on the spine saying which series they refer to. |

| | |
|---|---|
| *Introductory note* | An introduction to the contents of a series, explaining why the records were created, and what they contain. These exist for all medieval, early modern and legal series, for most very modern series, and for some other series.<br><br>They are usually printed on green paper, and are filed with the series lists in what is known as the Standard Set of series lists. This is the full set of paper lists, in alphabetical order. |
| *Calendar* | A précis, usually in English, full enough to replace the original documents for most purposes. The documents have been published in date order in many, but not all, calendars. |
| *Publications* | The PRO publishes readers' guides and handbooks. These are the specialist guides to particular records, referred to in this book. |
| *Transcript* | A full text. |
| *Index* | Alphabetically arranged references to people, places or subjects mentioned in the records. |

As well as the traditional methods described above, you now have the option of searching through the whole combined catalogue of the *Guide* (published for the last time in 1999) and lists on computer. The PRO on-line catalogue or PROCAT is accessible via the web and on site at Kew and at the FRC.

PROCAT is the Public Record Office's on-line multilevel catalogue containing over 9 million entries. The catalogue contains document descriptions, administrative histories of departments, series descriptions and the leaflets.

PROCAT is hierarchically arranged in seven levels:

Department (formerly Lettercode), e.g. HO
Division
Series (formerly Class), e.g. HO 45
Subseries
Sub-subseries
Piece, e.g. HO 45/2669
Item

PROCAT has a very powerful search engine, which allows you to search all catalogue descriptions by key word(s) and for many levels by date range. Once registered as a PRO reader you can bookmark entries of interest and save your searches.

**Using PROCAT**

From the public screen menu click on Catalogue and Document Ordering.

You can now enter the catalogue in two ways: as a registered reader or anonymously.

Registered reader: log on using your reader ticket. As a registered reader you have full access to the catalogue, your saved searches and bookmarked entries, and can order documents (provided you have a seat number).

Anonymous reader: you do not need a reader's ticket but you will only have access to the catalogue. If you wish to order documents or save your searches you need to log on with your reader's ticket.

Once you have logged on you can now click on one of the following:

Browse the catalogue – to access the catalogue, and for registered readers your personalised Home page.

Quick order (this is only available to Registered readers) – if you know the references of documents you wish to order and have a seat number click here.

Log off – to finish your session and return to the Catalogue and Document Ordering screen.

PROCAT is available on-line at http://catalogue.pro.gov.uk

As part of its e-business strategy, the Public Record Office is committed to making its most popular collections of records available on-line to increase accessibility to users. Already identified as candidates for the PRO on-line project are all of the decennial census returns 1841–1901, PCC Wills, Death Duty registers and Cabinet papers. At the time of publication it was not agreed when all of these records would be made available electronically, so check the PRO web site for the latest information.

The PRO Library and Resource Centre has excellent sets of periodicals and journals, for all kinds of history.

The Library has the indexes to *The Times* and the Parliamentary Papers (from 1801) on CD-ROM, as well as several other useful CD-ROMs. These can produce extraordinary amounts of information – the Parliamentary Papers in particular are full of details, and using the index on a key word search can turn up all kinds of published returns of people marginally involved in government, or giving evidence on subjects of social concern.

# Passenger Lists and Passports

The great age of passenger travel at sea came during the nineteenth and early twentieth centuries with the massive expansion of emigration and tourism. The main wave of emigration was to the USA and the reasons for emigrating have included the need to escape war, poverty, and religious and political persecution in search of a better life. It is estimated that since 1607 Great Britain and Ireland have sent well over 10 million emigrants to the USA, along with 4 million to Canada and 1.5 million to Australasia. Between 1845 and 1851 over 1.25 million Irish emigrated to the USA (mainly via Liverpool) as a result of the potato famine.

Shipping lines provided transport and cheap fares, although conditions were crowded and death from disease was rife. Travellers and tourists were initially carried by shipping companies as a sideline to more lucrative contracts, such as the transport of mail and merchandise between Europe, America and imperial possessions in India and Africa.

However, it was recognized that good passenger facilities brought status and increasing custom and large liners were built to transport emigrants. The wealthy travelled on the upper decks in first-class conditions, the poor on the lower decks in 'steerage' with communal cooking and living arrangements.

Between the 1840s and the 1930s, a combination of goods and mail transportation, tourism and migration fuelled the rise of famous shipping lines such as Cunard, Peninsular & Oriental Steam Navigation Company (P&O), the American White Star Line, the Norddeutscher Lloyd Line, and the French Compagnie Générale Transatlantique (CGT). The fiercely competitive and lucrative transatlantic trade grew rapidly. The dream of the emigrant was one of arrival in a country where – so it was said – land was free and fertile, religious and political dissent were tolerated, and class division did not exist. In the 1860s steamships started to replace sailing ships which cut the length of the journey time to North America from over four weeks to about eight days and to Australia from 10 to 17 weeks to four to six weeks. The 1855 Passenger Act helped to improve conditions, laying down minimum standards for rations, space and sanitation.

Emigration to the USA slowed with the introduction of new entry restrictions after 1918. Following the First World War other destinations such as Canada and Australia became increasingly popular, encouraged by governments both in the UK and in the Dominions/Commonwealth. *See* 2.1.3.

Surviving documents (published and unpublished) used to record the physical departure of emigrants are listed below. It should be noted that British sources are usually less full than those kept overseas and, unlike some overseas archives, there are no passenger lists in the PRO for civilian aircraft leaving or entering the UK.

## 1.1 Published sources

Many outwards passenger lists to America, Australasia and South Africa have been published, particularly those that date before 1800. Some publications have been compiled from primary sources within the PRO but most have been published using sources recording the arrival of emigrants in the destination countries. A number of known publications are listed in the Bibliography and many are available in the Research Enquiries Room or Library and Resource Centre. Many are particularly rich in source material.

For example, P W Filby and M K Meyer (ed.) *Passenger and Immigration Lists Index,* (Detroit, 1981 and annual supplements to 2000) is effectively a guide to published records of more than 3,340,000 immigrants who came to the New World between the sixteenth and mid-twentieth centuries. Entries within these volumes have been derived from a broad collection of more than 1,080 published passenger lists, naturalization records, church records and local histories, together with electoral lists and land registration records.

## 1.2 Port Books and passengers recorded before 1890

Most of the records of passengers leaving the UK are scattered among a variety of archives or have simply not survived. However, much material can be found at the destinations where the passengers became new citizens.

Generally speaking, emigration passenger lists between 1776–1889 have not survived. For the period before 1820, the Genealogical Society of Baltimore, USA, has reprinted all the surviving lists for vessels bound for North America and these include those for 1773–1776 in T 47 (*see* 1.2.3), as well as much of the material found at the destination ports in America. The PRO holds most of these listings and many of the sources are detailed in the Bibliography.

### 1.2.1 Port Books, 1565–1798

E 190: Exchequer: King's Remembrancer: Port Books, 1565–1798 were compiled as a result of an Exchequer Order of November 1564 requiring all customs officials in the various ports of England and Wales to make their entries in blank books issued by the Exchequer.

The books are of three kinds: entry books of the collectors and other officials, recording the details of cockets issued as receipts for the payment of the various duties on imports and exports; entry books of searchers, waiters and other officials who were concerned with shipping movements and the inspection of cargoes, not with the collection of duties; and coasting books, which record the issue and return of certificates for the transit of goods by coast from one English port to another. The certificates stated that the shippers had entered into bonds to unload only at another port within the realm.

Each entry in a Port Book generally contains the name of the ship and its master, the names of the merchants, a description of their goods, and, in the entry books of the collectors, the amount of duties paid. After 1600 most books contain details of the places to and from which shipments were made. Undoubtedly some of the exporters were also themselves emigrants, but there is no way of distinguishing between the two from the records. The records are not indexed by name though they have been used to compile many of the sources indicated in the Bibliography. The records are arranged by port and then by date. The ports named are those that were prosperous and prominent in early modern England and each 'headport' such as Chester also subsumes a number of at that time lesser ports such as Liverpool and Lancaster.

### 1.2.2 Registers of Passengers, 1634–77

Several registers of passengers travelling from a number of UK ports to New England, Barbados and other colonies for 1634–9, with one of 1677, can be found in E 157: Exchequer: King's Remembrancer: Registers of Licences to pass beyond the seas. The registers have been printed in J C Hotten *Original Lists of Persons Emigrating to America, 1600–1700* (London, 1874). For further information about E 157, *see* 1.4.1.

Lists of passengers, with names and ages, on board vessels bound for America in the 1630s can also be found in CO 1: Privy Council and related bodies: America and West Indies, Colonial Papers (General Series). These include CO 1/8, folios 100–102 displaying names of passengers bound for New England on board the *Francis* of Ipswich in 1634 and CO 1/9 folios 246–247, which includes names of passengers intended for New England on the *Confidence* in 1636–8.

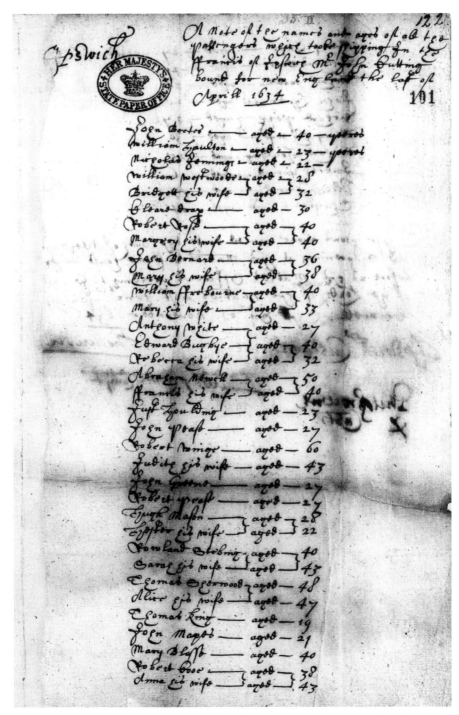

**Figure 1** List of passengers on board the *Francis* of Ipswich, bound for New England, 1634 (CO 1/8 (fol.100–102))

### 1.2.3  *Treasury Registers of Passengers, 1773–6*

A useful, though unfortunately short-lived, Treasury register (T 47/9–12) was kept by port customs officials of emigrants going from England, Wales and Scotland to the New World between 1773 and 1776. The information for England and Wales has been summarized in a card index, available in the Research Enquiries Room, which gives name, age, occupation, reason for leaving the country, last place of residence, date of departure and destination. This series also includes names of passengers to Europe.

### 1.2.4  *Shipping Line Emigration Lists, 1840–1909*

#### 1.2.4.1  Cunard and White Star Lines

From the middle of the seventeenth century, Liverpool was a major port for emigration to North America. Passengers, some of whom were indentured servants, others simply emigrants seeking a better life elsewhere, were attracted to Liverpool from throughout the British Isles (not just the north west of England). Later, in the nineteenth century, with the attraction of North Sea steamers and railway links across England, Liverpool attracted emigrants from mainland Europe who would travel from the ports of Hamburg or Bremen to Hull and then make their way across to Liverpool by train to board a ship for America. By 1851, Liverpool was the prime migrant port of Europe sending approximately 160,000 passengers to America in that year alone and during the period 1830 to 1930 it is estimated that over 9 million emigrants left Liverpool in search of a new life. By the 1860s, Liverpool began regular voyages to Australia and New Zealand, though these destinations proved popular from other UK ports, particularly London and Southampton and, to a lesser extent, Bristol.

Cunard, White Star, Allan, Inmar, Guion, and National Lines all sailed from Liverpool, though many refused to carry passengers until the 1860s.

By the late nineteenth century, Liverpool's dominant role was being challenged, particularly by German ports such as Bremen and Hamburg but also by Southampton. The position of Liverpool was further weakened in 1926 when restrictions on immigration were imposed by the USA.

The University of Liverpool, Liverpool L69 3BX, has in its archives a small selection of outward passenger lists from the Cunard and White Star Shipping Lines. Very few passenger lists are included in their archive but those which are cover the period 1840 to 1909 for voyages to Canada and the USA. For example, the University has three microfilms of passenger lists of the Cunard Line for the period 1840–53.

The Merseyside Maritime Museum Library and Archives, Albert Dock, Liverpool, hold diaries and letters of emigrants, family history notes and other official documents and correspondence including selected passenger lists and surgeons' reports.

No records of 'exit passes' of passengers or passenger application forms are known to survive in any UK archive.

### 1.2.4.2 P&O Shipping Line

No shipping line passenger lists appear to survive for the port of London for the period before 1890. Although P&O (Peninsular and Oriental) Shipping Line has lodged its archives with the National Maritime Museum, Maritime Information Centre, Romney Road, London SE10 9NF, only a very small sample of lists has survived for voyages after 1890 and Board of Trade copies of these lists can be found in BT 27: Outwards Passenger Lists, *see* 1.3.1.

### *1.2.5 Births, marriages and deaths of passengers at sea*

There was no legal requirement to list passengers on board British vessels prior to the Merchant Shipping Act 1894, though following the Merchant Shipping Act 1854, registers were compiled, from ships' official logs, of births, deaths and marriages of passengers at sea.

Most emigrants travelled in the cheapest class of accommodation, known as steerage. The accommodation was frequently overcrowded and with poor ventilation, diseases such as cholera and typhus reached epidemic proportions and many emigrants died as a result, particularly prior to the 1870s (by which time virtually all emigrants to North America and most to Australia travelled by steamship which helped to cut journey times considerably). From about 1900 third class cabins replaced steerage accommodation and although they were spartan, this was a considerable improvement.

Births, marriages and deaths are all recorded from 1854–83, births and deaths only from 1883–87 and deaths only from 1888 to 1890. These records are in the series BT 158: Registers of Births, Deaths and Marriages of Passengers at Sea. Masters were further required by the Registration of Births and Deaths Act 1874 to report births and deaths of both United Kingdom subjects and aliens to the Registrar General of Shipping: the information about United Kingdom subjects is in the series BT 160: Registers of Births of British Nationals at Sea 1875–1891 and BT 159: Registers of Deaths of British Nationals at Sea 1875–1888. Records of births and deaths at sea, 1891–1964 are held in BT 334 with a marriage register for 1854–1972.

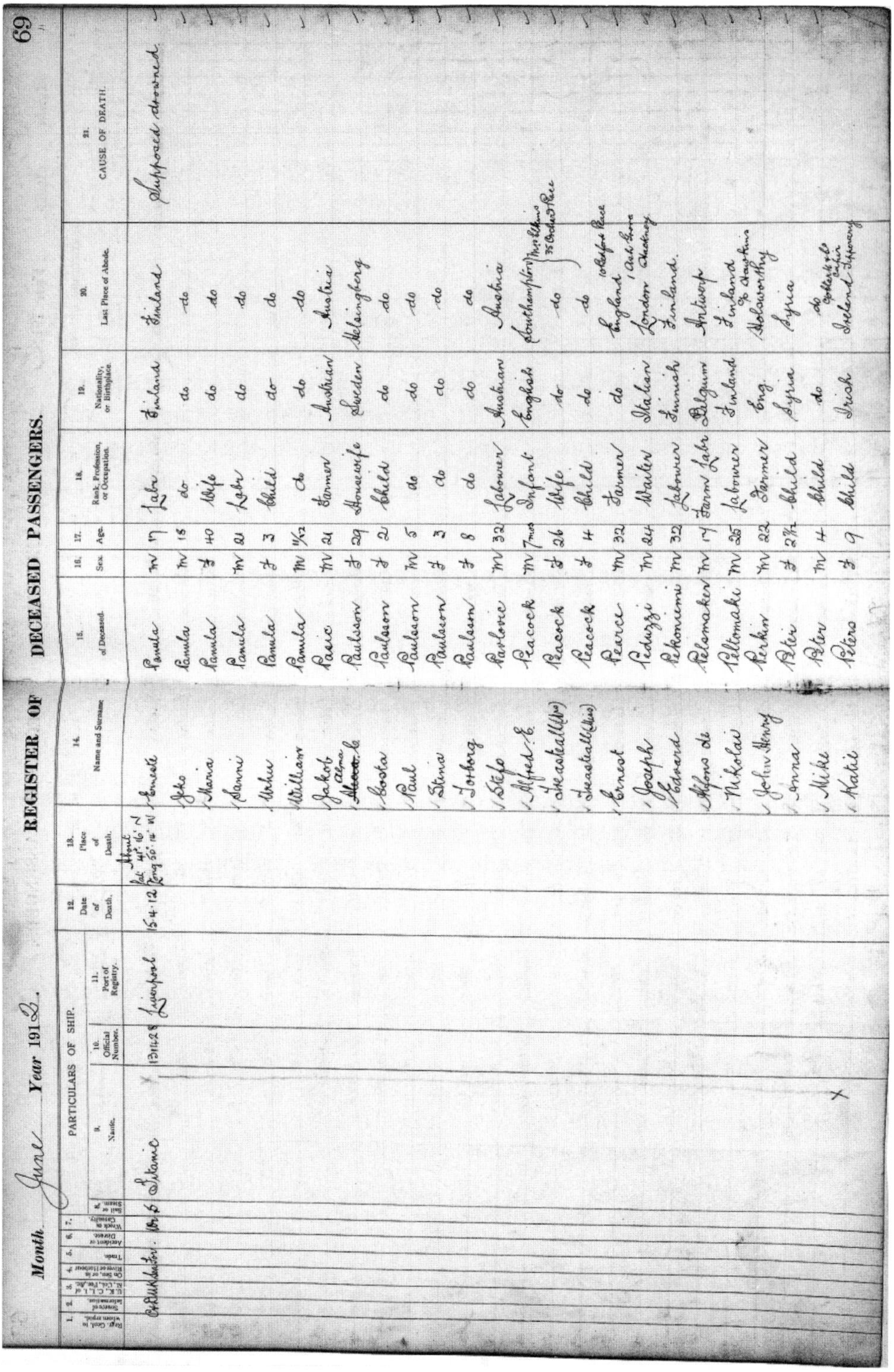

69

REGISTER OF DECEASED PASSENGERS.

Month June Year 1912.

| 9. Name (of ship) | 10. Official Number | 11. Port of Registry | 12. Date of Death | 13. Place of Death | 14. Name and Surname | 15. of Deceased | 16. Sex | 17. Age | 18. Rank, Profession, or Occupation | 19. Nationality, or Birthplace | 20. Last Place of Abode | 21. Cause of Death |
|---|---|---|---|---|---|---|---|---|---|---|---|---|
| Titanic | 131428 | Liverpool | 15.4.12 | About Lat 41°16' N Long 50°14' W | Ernesti | Panula | M | 17 | Labr | Finland | Finland | Supposed drowned |
| | | | | | Jako | Panula | M | 15 | do | do | do | |
| | | | | | Maria | Panula | F | 40 | Wife | do | do | |
| | | | | | Janni | Panula | M | 21 | Labr | do | do | |
| | | | | | Urhu | Panula | F | 3 | Child | do | do | |
| | | | | | William | Panula | M | 11/12 | do | do | do | |
| | | | | | Jakob | Pasic | M | 21 | Farmer | Austrian | Austria | |
| | | | | | Alma C | Paulsson | F | 29 | Housewife | Sweden | Helsingborg | |
| | | | | | Gosta | Paulsson | F | 2 | Child | do | do | |
| | | | | | Paul | Paulsson | M | 5 | do | do | do | |
| | | | | | Stina | Paulsson | F | 3 | do | do | do | |
| | | | | | Torborg | Paulsson | F | 8 | do | do | do | |
| | | | | | Stefo | Pavlovic | M | 32 | Labourer | Austrian | Austria | |
| | | | | | Alfred E. | Peacock | M | 7 mos | Infant | English | Southampton } Mrs Elkins 35 Orchard Place | |
| | | | | | Treasteall (Mrs) | Peacock | F | 26 | Wife | do | do | |
| | | | | | Treasteall (Miss) | Peacock | F | 4 | Child | do | do | |
| | | | | | Ernest | Pearce | M | 32 | Farmer | do | England 10 Oxford Place | |
| | | | | | Joseph | Peduzzi | M | 24 | Waiter | Italian | London 1 Ash Grove Hackney | |
| | | | | | Edward | Pekoniemi | M | 32 | Labourer | Finnish | Finland. | |
| | | | | | Alfons de | Pelsmaker | M | 17 | Farm Labr | Belgium | Antwerp | |
| | | | | | Nikolai | Peltomaki | M | 25 | Labourer | Finland | Finland | |
| | | | | | John Henry | Perkin | M | 22 | Farmer | Eng. | Holsworthy c/o Hawkins | |
| | | | | | Anna | Peter | F | 2½ | Child | Syria | Syria | |
| | | | | | Mike | Peter | M | 4 | Child | do | do | |
| | | | | | Katie | Peters | F | 9 | Child | Irish | Ireland Tipperary | |

**Figure 2** Register of Deceased Passengers, April 1912. Entry for RMS *Titanic* (BT 334/52)

Colonial Office returns of some births and deaths at sea are discussed in 5.2.5.

The FRC holds births and deaths at sea (marine) of British people registered from July 1837 to 1965. Civil aviation births and deaths and missing (presumed dead) from 1947 to 1965 are also available at the FRC. From 1966 all births, marriages and deaths at sea and registered by the UK High Commissions and consuls abroad are indexed in union volumes for each type of event. These records are discussed in greater detail in Chapter 5.

## 1.3 Board of Trade Passenger Lists, 1890–1960

The Merchant Shipping Act 1894 (57&58 Victoria, c 60) required the listing of passengers on board British merchant vessels. Ships' passenger lists among the records of the Board of Trade relate mainly to arrivals in and departures from UK seaports. The lists were deposited with the Board of Trade by the various passenger shipping lines. BT 27 are Passenger Lists: Outwards.

To find your document you should know the first port of departure from the UK and the date of departure. Some ports are not named separately, but included with other ports nearby; see the explanatory note at the front of the BT 27 series list for details. Some ports are also known by different names, e.g. Queenstown = Cork. If you do not know the port of departure, but do know the name of the ship, you could use the Registers of Passenger Lists, 1906–1951, in BT 32 – *see* 1.3.2. If you do not know the port of departure or name of ship, it will be very difficult and time consuming to find any record.

Many passenger lists are in a fragile condition, and searching them can be very time consuming. There are no indexes of names, and most lists are not alphabetical. The information given varies, but can include age, address in UK (from 1922) and occupation. Lists after the 1930s indicate whether or not passengers were travelling for tourist/leisure reasons. There are separate lists for British and alien passengers. These records are delivered in the Map and Large Document Room.

Shipping Line copies of a very small selection of passenger lists can be found at other archives. For the P&O shipping line, contact the National Maritime Museum, Greenwich, London SE10 9NF (*see* 1.2.4.2), and for Cunard and White Star shipping line passenger lists, contact the University of Liverpool, Liverpool L69 3BX (*see* 1.2.4.1).

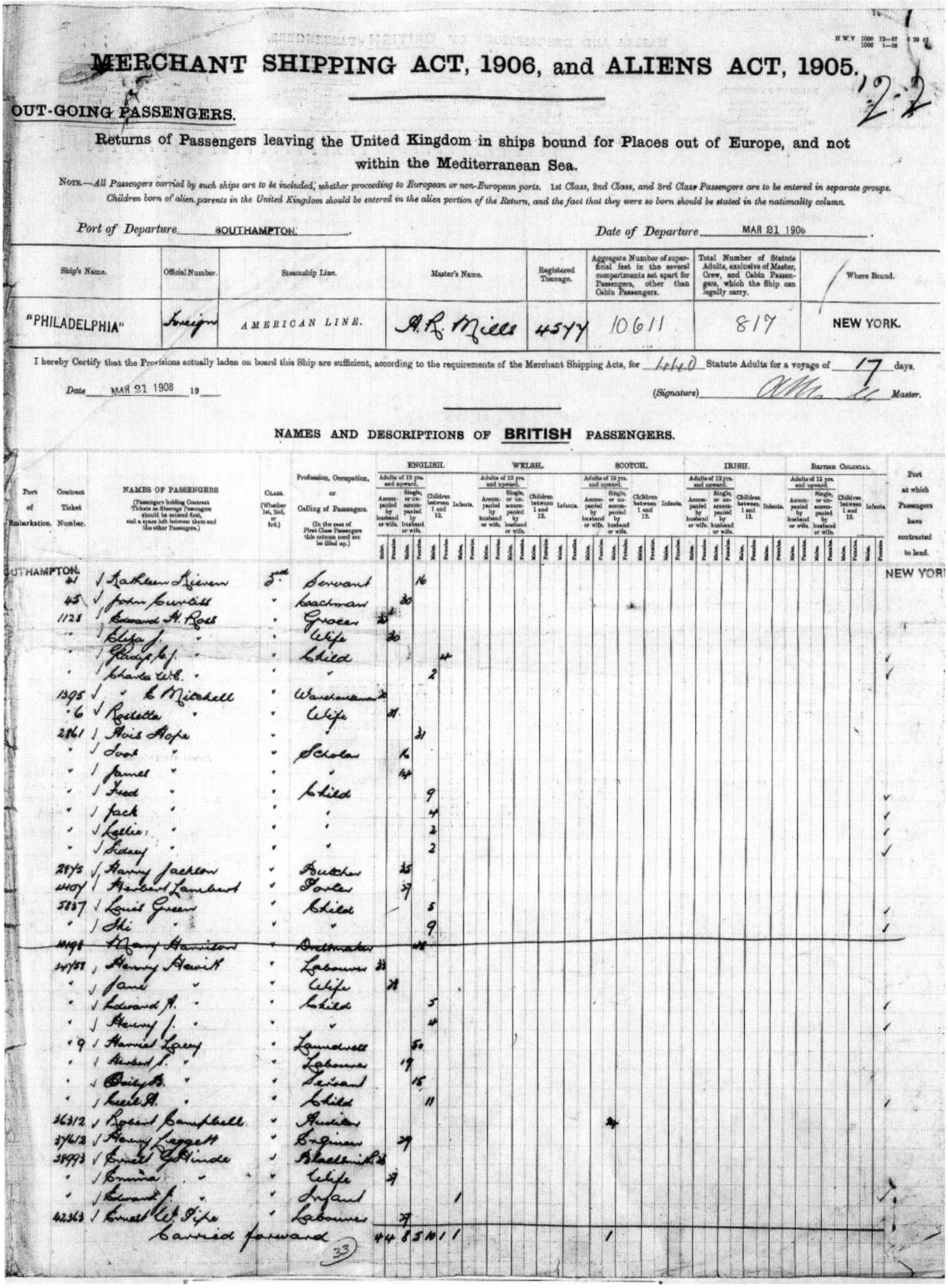
MERCHANT SHIPPING ACT, 1906, and ALIENS ACT, 1905.

OUT-GOING PASSENGERS.

Returns of Passengers leaving the United Kingdom in ships bound for Places out of Europe, and not within the Mediterranean Sea.

NOTE.—All Passengers carried by such ships are to be included, whether proceeding to European or non-European ports. 1st Class, 2nd Class, and 3rd Class Passengers are to be entered in separate groups. Children born of alien parents in the United Kingdom should be entered in the alien portion of the Return, and the fact that they were so born should be stated in the nationality column.

Port of Departure SOUTHAMPTON. Date of Departure MAR 21 1908.

| Ship's Name. | Official Number. | Steamship Line. | Master's Name. | Registered Tonnage. | Aggregate Number of superficial feet in the several compartments set apart for Passengers, other than Cabin Passengers. | Total Number of Statute Adults, exclusive of Master, Crew, and Cabin Passengers, which the Ship can legally carry. | Where Bound. |
|---|---|---|---|---|---|---|---|
| "PHILADELPHIA" | Foreign | AMERICAN LINE. | A. R. Mills | 4577 | 10611 | 817 | NEW YORK. |

I hereby Certify that the Provisions actually laden on board this Ship are sufficient, according to the requirements of the Merchant Shipping Acts, for 1460 Statute Adults for a voyage of 17 days.

Date MAR 21 1908 19__ (Signature) A. R. Mills Master.

NAMES AND DESCRIPTIONS OF BRITISH PASSENGERS.

| Port of Embarkation. | Contract Ticket Number. | Names of Passengers | Class. | Profession, Occupation, or Calling of Passengers. | Age (English) | Port at which Passengers have contracted to land. |
|---|---|---|---|---|---|---|
| SOUTHAMPTON. | 41 | Kathleen Kiernan | 3rd | Servant | 16 | NEW YORK |
| | 45 | John Curtiss | " | Coachman | 30 | |
| | 1128 | Edward H. Ross | " | Grocer | 30 | |
| | " | Eliza J. " | " | Wife | 30 | |
| | " | Gladys M. " | " | Child | 4 | |
| | " | Charles W. E. " | " | " | 2 | |
| | 1395 | " C. Mitchell | " | Warehouseman | 30 | |
| | "6 | Rosetta " | " | Wife | 31 | |
| | 2861 | Avis Hope | " | | 31 | |
| | " | Ivor " | " | Scholar | 16 | |
| | " | James " | " | " | 14 | |
| | " | Fred " | " | Child | 9 | |
| | " | Jack " | " | | 4 | |
| | " | Leslie " | " | | 2 | |
| | " | Sidney " | " | | 2 | |
| | 2875 | Harry Jackson | " | Butcher | 35 | |
| | 4407 | Herbert Lambert | " | Porter | 37 | |
| | 5887 | Louis Green | " | Child | 5 | |
| | " | Ethel " | " | " | 9 | |
| | ~~4498~~ | ~~Mary Hamilton~~ | " | ~~Dressmaker~~ | ~~48~~ | |
| | 34/51 | Henry Hewitt | " | Labourer | 33 | |
| | " | Jane " | " | Wife | 38 | |
| | " | Edward A. " | " | Child | 5 | |
| | " | Henry J. " | " | " | 4 | |
| | "9 | Harriet Lacey | " | Laundress | 50 | |
| | " | Herbert J. " | " | Labourer | 19 | |
| | " | Emily B. " | " | Servant | 15 | |
| | " | Lucie A. " | " | Child | 11 | |
| | 36312 | Robert Campbell | " | Auditor | 34 | |
| | 37612 | Henry Leggett | " | Engineer | 29 | |
| | 38993 | Ernest G. Hinde | " | Blacksmith | 28 | |
| | " | Emma " | " | Wife | 27 | |
| | " | Edward J. " | " | Infant | 1 | |
| | 42363 | Ernest W. Pipe | " | Labourer | 27 | |
| | | Carried forward | | | 44 8 5 10 1 1 … 1 | |

Figure 3 Passenger List outwards, 21 March 1908, Southampton: includes on the vessel *Philadelphia*, the passengers Leslie (Bob) Hope, his mother, and five brothers (BT 27/594)

### 1.3.1 Outwards Lists, 1890–1960 (BT 27)

BT 27 contains the 'Passenger Lists, Outwards' from 1890. Earlier lists have not survived.

These give the names of all passengers leaving the UK, where the ship's eventual destination was a port outside Europe and the Mediterranean Sea. However, names of passengers who disembarked at European ports and transmigrants will be included in these lists. Passenger lists for ships whose voyages both began and ended within Europe (including the UK and the Mediterranean) are not included. Although there are no indexes of names and most lists are not alphabetical, DataMarine has extracted almost 50,000 names and details from some Board of Trade passenger lists for Australia-bound vessels for the years 1909–14, when thousands of British people chose to emigrate. They have also produced finding aids for locating lists in BT 27. DataMarine can be contacted via e-mail at marine@netcomuk.co.uk.

Passenger Lists: Inwards are in BT 26 and are very similar to BT 27 in scope and content. The records are arranged by date and final port of destination (arrival) in the UK.

Passenger lists do not survive after 1960 when travel by air became more popular. No air passenger lists have been preserved, though records of civil aviation births and deaths of passengers are available at the FRC (*see* 1.2.5).

### 1.3.2 Registers and Directories of Passenger Lists

BT 32 contains names of ships for which passenger lists exist in BT 27. The entries are not complete however – the earliest years have entries for a few ports only and there are omissions. For readers hoping to find the name of a passenger in BT 27, they are of limited use, and may only be helpful if the name of the ship is already known. They do not contain the names of passengers, nor the destination of ships. These records are on open access in the Research Enquiries Room.

Available at the Research Enquiries Room desk, *The Morton Allan Directory of European Passenger Steamship Arrivals* (Genealogical Publishing Co., Inc, 1993) contains listings of the arrivals of passenger steamships at New York for 1890–30 and Philadelphia, Boston and Baltimore for 1904–1930. The directory is arranged by year and alphabetically indexed by steamship line. The port of arrival and port of departure are shown at the top of each entry. As with BT 32, the Directory does not contain the names of passengers but provides clues as to where passengers may have sailed from in a particular year and is of immense help if the name of the vessel is already known, but the port of departure is not.

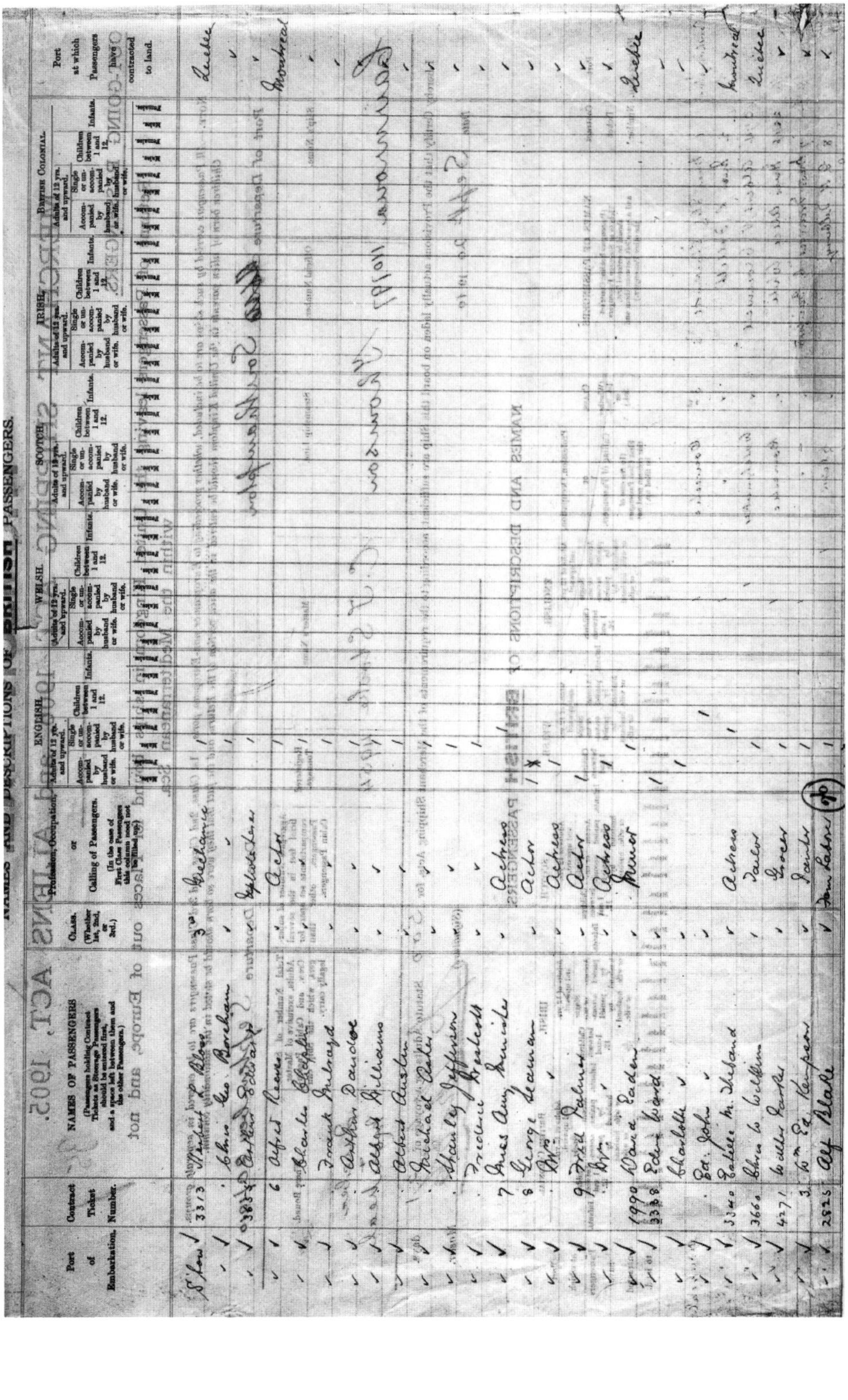

**Figure 4** Passenger List outwards, 20 September 1910, Southampton–Quebec and Montreal: includes on SS *Cairnrona*, the passengers Charles Chaplin and Stanley Jefferson (Stan Laurel) (BT 27/688)

## 1.4  Passenger Lists held in overseas archives

Inwards ships' passenger lists and passenger cards provide a valuable source of genealogical information, especially if no corresponding outwards passenger list survives from UK archives. These records tend to be arranged chronologically and by port of arrival and few name indexes survive for twentieth-century lists.

There are useful web sites for passenger lists, often containing transcripts of lists themselves. Examples of these include:

> www.theshipslist.com for ship passenger lists
>
> http://home.att.net/~arnielang/shipgide.html the immigration and ships' passenger lists research guide
>
> www.genealogy.com/genealogy/8_mgpal.html for locating ships' passenger lists
>
> http://home.att.net/~wee-monster/onlinelists.html for Internet sources for transcribed passenger records and indexes
>
> http://home.att.net/~wee-monster/ei.html for emigration and immigration link
>
> www.blaxland.com/ozships Australian arrivals and departures 1788–1967
>
> http://freepages.genealogy.rootsweb.com/~britishhomechildren/the essential site for researching the British 'Home Children' who were sent to Canada between 1870 and 1940
>
> www.standard.net.au/~jwilliams/ships.htm an index of ships 1829–1900, with information from various newspapers
>
> www.ellisisland.org to search on-line over 22 million passengers and members of the ships' crews who came through Ellis Island and the Port of New York between 1892 and 1924
>
> http://istg.rootsweb.com find your immigrant ancestors
>
> www.hamburg.de/LinkToYourRoots/english/welcome.htm if you think your ancestors emigrated from Europe to the New World via Hamburg
>
> http://olivetreegenealogy.com/index.shtml passenger lists and much information about ships
>
> www.beavis.co.uk/pslist.htm for 50,000 names and details from some Board of Trade passenger lists for Australia-bound vessels for the years 1909–14

### 1.4.1  Australia

Passenger lists for all ports in Australia survive from 1924, with some gaps. Earlier inwards passenger lists survive for the ports of Newcastle (for 1865–84), Darwin (1898–1934), Bowen (1897–1962), Brisbane (1852–1964), Cairns (from 1897), Hobart (from 1903), Rockhampton (from 1898) Townsville (from 1895), Fremantle/Perth (from 1898). Further information is available at the National Archives of Australia web site at www.naa.gov.au.

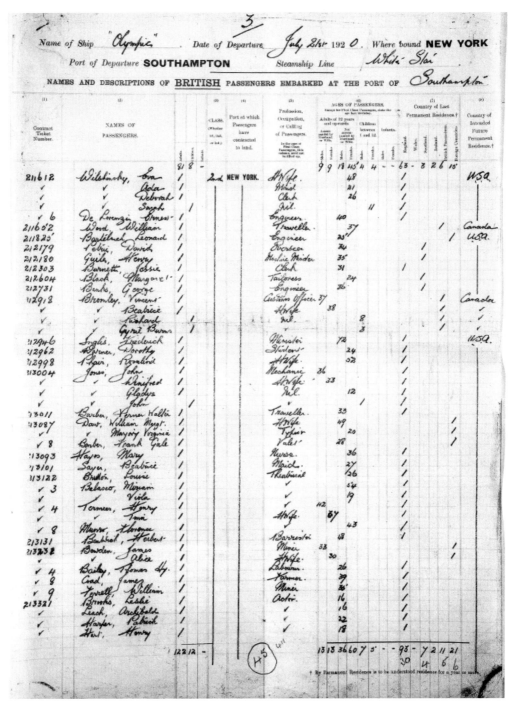

**Figure 5** Passenger List outwards, July 1920, Southampton: includes the passengers from SS *Olympia* (ON 131346) including one Archibald Leach who became Hollywood actor Cary Grant (BT 27/931)

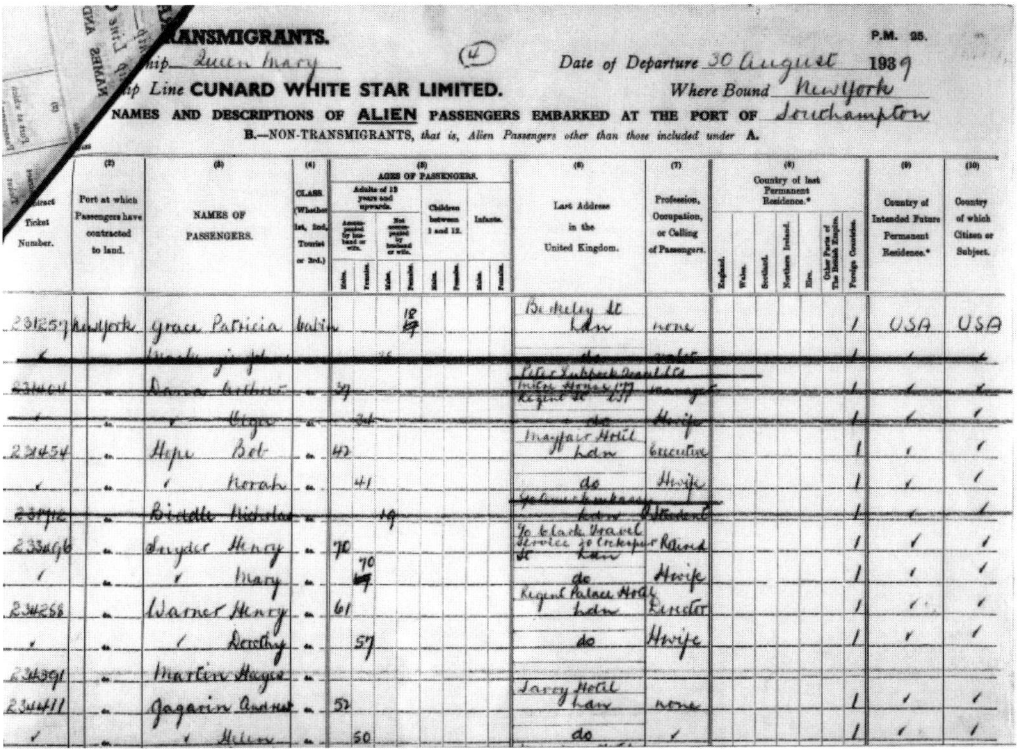
ANSMIGRANTS. P.M. 25.
Ship Queen Mary (4) Date of Departure 30 August 1939
Line CUNARD WHITE STAR LIMITED. Where Bound New York
NAMES AND DESCRIPTIONS OF ALIEN PASSENGERS EMBARKED AT THE PORT OF Southampton
B.—NON-TRANSMIGRANTS, that is, Alien Passengers other than those included under A.

| Ticket Number | Port at which Passengers have contracted to land | Names of Passengers | Class | Ages of Passengers | Last Address in the United Kingdom | Profession, Occupation, or Calling of Passengers | Country of Intended Future Permanent Residence | Country of which Citizen or Subject |
|---|---|---|---|---|---|---|---|---|
| 231257 | New York | Grace Patricia | Cabin | 18 | Berkeley St Ldn | none | USA | USA |
| 231454 | " | Hope Bob | " | 42 | Mayfair Hotel Ldn | Executive | " | " |
| " | " | " Norah | " | 41 | do | Wife | " | " |
| 233496 | " | Snyder Henry | " | 70 | To black Travel Service 30 Cockspur St Ldn | Retired | " | " |
| " | " | " Mary | " | 70 | do | Wife | " | " |
| 234266 | " | Warner Henry | " | 61 | Regent Palace Hotel Ldn | Director | " | " |
| " | " | " Dorothy | " | 57 | do | Wife | " | " |
| 234391 | " | Martin Hayes | " | | | | | |
| 234411 | " | Gagarin Andrew | " | 52 | Savoy Hotel Ldn | none | " | " |
| " | " | " Helen | " | 50 | do | " | " | " |

**Figure 6** Passenger List outwards, August 1939, Southampton: includes the passengers from SS *Queen Mary*, including film actor Bob Hope (BT 27/1549). From 1922 lists include details of last UK address.

The Western Australian Genealogical Society (WAGS) is preparing a computer database of passengers, crew and stowaways on ships coming to and/or passing through Fremantle and/or other Western Australian ports for the years 1880–1925. The index will be released progressively to researchers at the WAGS library in Perth.

Inward air passenger lists generally survive from 1934 and, as with the ships' passenger lists, these records tend to be held at the state archives for the state in which the port of arrival is located.

Passenger lists in Australia are publicly available once they are 30 years old.

The useful web site entitled Convictions (www.blaxland.com/ozships/), lists Australian shipping arrivals and departures, 1788 to 1967. These pages were designed primarily to assist those who are interested in family history and genealogy. Besides containing shipping arrival details for various ports around Australia, they also include passenger lists and occasional crew list details for some of the ships.

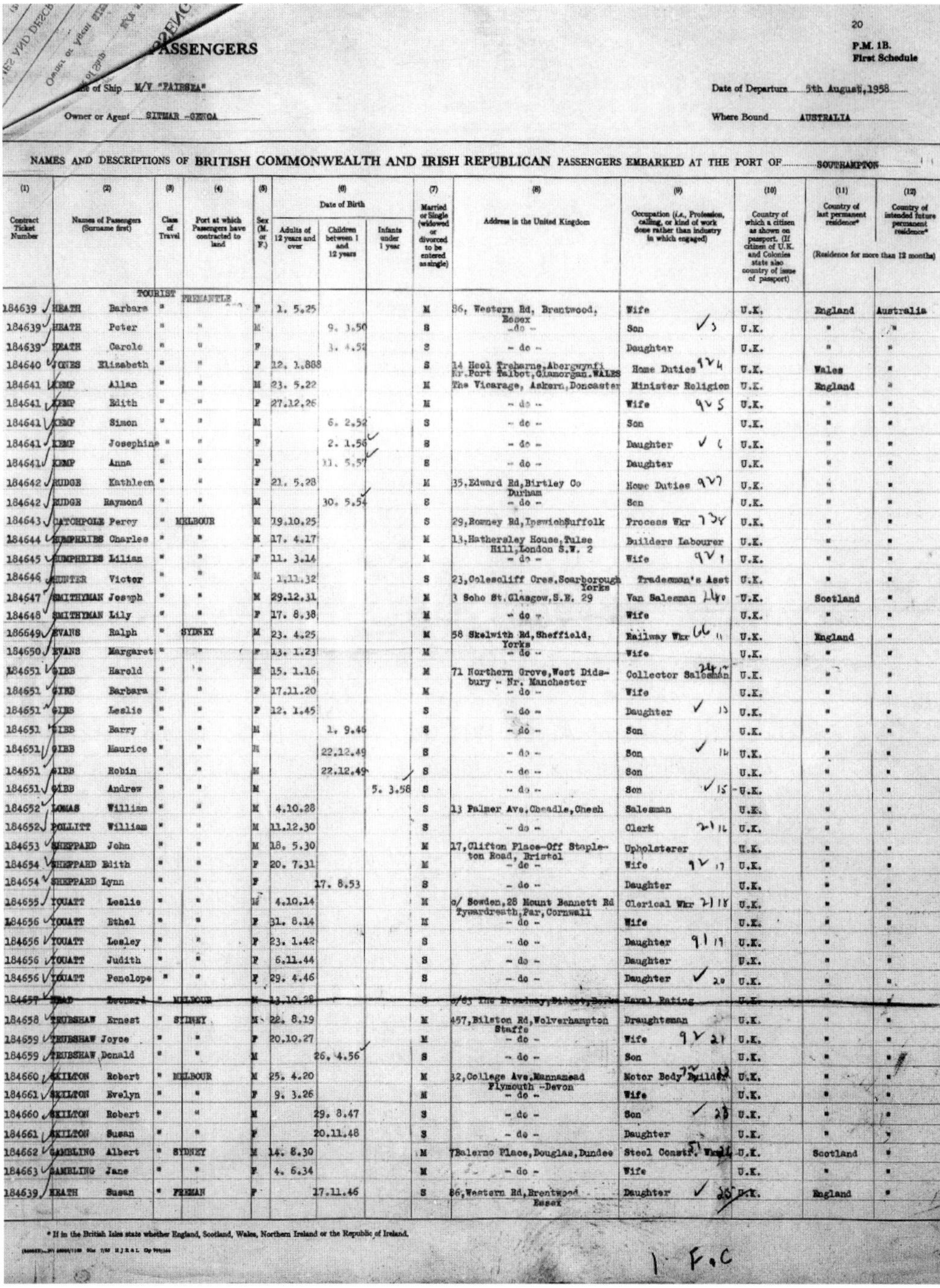

PASSENGERS

20

P.M. 1B.
First Schedule

Name of Ship M/V "FAIRSEA"

Owner or Agent SITMAR - GENOA

Date of Departure 5th August, 1958

Where Bound AUSTRALIA

NAMES AND DESCRIPTIONS OF BRITISH COMMONWEALTH AND IRISH REPUBLICAN PASSENGERS EMBARKED AT THE PORT OF SOUTHAMPTON

| (1) Contract Ticket Number | (2) Names of Passengers (Surname first) | (3) Class of Travel | (4) Port at which Passengers have contracted to land | (5) Sex (M. or F.) | (6) Date of Birth: Adults of 12 years and over | Children between 1 and 12 years | Infants under 1 year | (7) Married or Single (widowed or divorced to be entered as single) | (8) Address in the United Kingdom | (9) Occupation (i.e., Profession, calling, or kind of work done rather than industry in which engaged) | (10) Country of which a citizen as shown on passport. (If citizen of U.K. and Colonies state also country of issue of passport) | (11) Country of last permanent residence* (Residence for more than 12 months) | (12) Country of intended future permanent residence* |
|---|---|---|---|---|---|---|---|---|---|---|---|---|---|
| 184639 | HEATH Barbara | TOURIST | FREMANTLE | F | 1. 5.25 | | | M | 86, Western Rd, Brentwood, Essex | Wife | U.K. | England | Australia |
| 184639 | HEATH Peter | " | " | M | | 9. 3.50 | | S | -do- | Son | U.K. | " | " |
| 184639 | HEATH Carole | " | " | F | | 3. 4.52 | | S | - do - | Daughter | U.K. | " | " |
| 184640 | JONES Elizabeth | " | " | F | 12. 1.888 | | | S | 14 Heol Treharne, Abergwynfi Nr. Port Talbot, Glamorgan. WALES | Home Duties | U.K. | Wales | " |
| 184641 | KEMP Allan | " | " | M | 23. 5.22 | | | M | The Vicarage, Askern, Doncaster | Minister Religion | U.K. | England | " |
| 184641 | KEMP Edith | " | " | F | 27.12.26 | | | M | - do - | Wife | U.K. | " | " |
| 184641 | KEMP Simon | " | " | M | | 6. 2.52 | | S | - do - | Son | U.K. | " | " |
| 184641 | KEMP Josephine | " | " | F | | 2. 1.56 | | S | - do - | Daughter | U.K. | " | " |
| 184641 | KEMP Anna | " | " | F | | 11. 5.57 | | S | - do - | Daughter | U.K. | " | " |
| 184642 | RUDGE Kathleen | " | " | F | 21. 5.28 | | | M | 35, Edward Rd, Birtley Co Durham | Home Duties | U.K. | " | " |
| 184642 | RUDGE Raymond | " | " | M | | 30. 5.54 | | S | - do - | Son | U.K. | " | " |
| 184643 | CATCHPOLE Percy | " | MELBOUR | M | 19.10.25 | | | S | 29, Romney Rd, Ipswich Suffolk | Process Wkr | U.K. | " | " |
| 184644 | HUMPHRIES Charles | " | " | M | 17. 4.17 | | | M | 13, Hathersley House, Tulse Hill, London S.W. 2 | Builders Labourer | U.K. | " | " |
| 184645 | HUMPHRIES Lilian | " | " | F | 11. 3.14 | | | M | - do - | Wife | U.K. | " | " |
| 184646 | HUNTER Victor | " | " | M | 1.11.32 | | | S | 23, Colescliff Cres. Scarborough Yorks | Tradesman's Asst | U.K. | " | " |
| 184647 | SMITHYMAN Joseph | " | " | M | 29.12.31 | | | M | 3 Soho St. Glasgow, S.E. 29 | Van Salesman | U.K. | Scotland | " |
| 184648 | SMITHYMAN Lily | " | " | F | 17. 8.38 | | | M | - do - | Wife | U.K. | " | " |
| 186649 | EVANS Ralph | " | SYDNEY | M | 23. 4.25 | | | M | 58 Skelwith Rd, Sheffield, Yorks | Railway Wkr | U.K. | England | " |
| 184650 | EVANS Margaret | " | " | F | 13. 1.23 | | | M | - do - | Wife | U.K. | " | " |
| 184651 | GIBB Harold | " | " | M | 15. 1.16 | | | M | 71 Northern Grove, West Didsbury - Nr. Manchester | Collector Salesman | U.K. | " | " |
| 184651 | GIBB Barbara | " | " | F | 17.11.20 | | | M | - do - | Wife | U.K. | " | " |
| 184651 | GIBB Leslie | " | " | F | 12. 1.45 | | | S | - do - | Daughter | U.K. | " | " |
| 184651 | GIBB Barry | " | " | M | | 1. 9.46 | | S | - do - | Son | U.K. | " | " |
| 184651 | GIBB Maurice | " | " | M | | 22.12.49 | | S | - do - | Son | U.K. | " | " |
| 184651 | GIBB Robin | " | " | M | | 22.12.49 | | S | - do - | Son | U.K. | " | " |
| 184651 | GIBB Andrew | " | " | M | | | 5. 3.58 | S | - do - | Son | U.K. | " | " |
| 184652 | LOMAS William | " | " | M | 4.10.28 | | | S | 13 Palmer Ave, Cheadle, Chesh | Salesman | U.K. | " | " |
| 184652 | POLLITT William | " | " | M | 11.12.30 | | | S | - do - | Clerk | U.K. | " | " |
| 184653 | SHEPPARD John | " | " | M | 18. 5.30 | | | M | 17, Clifton Place-Off Stapleton Road, Bristol | Upholsterer | U.K. | " | " |
| 184654 | SHEPPARD Edith | " | " | F | 20. 7.31 | | | M | - do - | Wife | U.K. | " | " |
| 184654 | SHEPPARD Lynn | " | " | F | | 17. 8.53 | | S | - do - | Daughter | U.K. | " | " |
| 184655 | YOUATT Leslie | " | " | M | 4.10.14 | | | M | c/ Sowden, 28 Mount Bennett Rd Tywardreath, Par, Cornwall | Clerical Wkr | U.K. | " | " |
| 184656 | YOUATT Ethel | " | " | F | 31. 8.14 | | | M | - do - | Wife | U.K. | " | " |
| 184656 | YOUATT Lesley | " | " | F | 23. 1.42 | | | S | - do - | Daughter | U.K. | " | " |
| 184656 | YOUATT Judith | " | " | F | 6.11.44 | | | S | - do - | Daughter | U.K. | " | " |
| 184656 | YOUATT Penelope | " | " | F | 29. 4.46 | | | S | - do - | Daughter | U.K. | " | " |
| ~~184657~~ | ~~[illegible]~~ | ~~"~~ | ~~MELBOUR~~ | ~~M~~ | ~~13.10.28~~ | | | ~~S~~ | ~~c/65 The Broadway, Didcot, Berks~~ | ~~Naval Rating~~ | ~~U.K.~~ | ~~"~~ | ~~"~~ |
| 184658 | TRUBSHAW Ernest | " | SYDNEY | M | 22. 8.19 | | | M | 457, Bilston Rd, Wolverhampton Staffs | Draughtsman | U.K. | " | " |
| 184659 | TRUBSHAW Joyce | " | " | F | 20.10.27 | | | M | - do - | Wife | U.K. | " | " |
| 184659 | TRUBSHAW Donald | " | " | M | | 26. 4.56 | | S | - do - | Son | U.K. | " | " |
| 184660 | SKILTON Robert | " | MELBOUR | M | 25. 4.20 | | | M | 32, College Ave. Mannamead Plymouth - Devon | Motor Body Builder | U.K. | " | " |
| 184661 | SKILTON Evelyn | " | " | F | 9. 3.26 | | | M | - do - | Wife | U.K. | " | " |
| 184660 | SKILTON Robert | " | " | M | | 29. 8.47 | | S | - do - | Son | U.K. | " | " |
| 184661 | SKILTON Susan | " | " | F | | 20.11.48 | | S | - do - | Daughter | U.K. | " | " |
| 184662 | GAMBLING Albert | " | SYDNEY | M | 14. 8.30 | | | M | 7 Balerno Place, Douglas, Dundee | Steel Constr. Wkr | U.K. | Scotland | " |
| 184663 | GAMBLING Jane | " | " | F | 4. 6.34 | | | M | - do - | Wife | U.K. | " | " |
| 184639 | HEATH Susan | " | FREMAN | F | | 17.11.46 | | S | 86, Western Rd, Brentwood Essex | Daughter | U.K. | England | " |

* If in the British Isles state whether England, Scotland, Wales, Northern Ireland or the Republic of Ireland.

1 F.C

**Figure 7** Passenger List outwards, August 1958, Southampton: includes the passengers from SS *Fairsea* including Barry, Robin and Maurice Gibb (the Bee Gees) who emigrated to Australia as part of the New Life emigration scheme (BT 27/1851)

In addition to these details, this site also contains a number of background pages covering a small number of shipwreck details and other information such as passenger diaries.

The main shipping pages contain some 31,000 entries covering all ports from 1788 to 1967. Each entry contains the name of the ship, the arrival or departure date, port of origin and destination, if known, plus other details. If there is a passenger diary, passenger list, crew list or convict list for the ship, it may also be reached from this site via hyperlinks. Note that although almost all of the information is relevant to Australia, there are occasional entries for other countries, especially for people bound for New Zealand.

### 1.4.2 New Zealand

For New Zealand, from 1883 onwards, the web site http://members.nbci.com/_XMCM/DenisePeter/OurStuff.htm contains information relating to inwards passenger lists for nearly all ships. The original passenger lists are held by Archives New Zealand at 10 Mulgrove Street, Thorndon, PO Box 120150, Wellington, New Zealand (web site: www.archives.govt.nz/index.htm). These lists were compiled by shipping companies and handed to a customs officer when the ship first arrived in New Zealand. The amount of information contained on these passenger lists varies though most lists include the person's surname and initial, age, occupation and nationality. Lists prior to 1910 for the ports of Wellington, Auckland and Lyttelton and Bluff have been indexed by name though those beyond 1910 have not and these lists are arranged chronologically and by port of arrival.

### 1.4.3 Canada

For Canada, there are no comprehensive nominal lists of immigrants arriving prior to 1865. Until that year, shipping companies were not required by the government to retain their passenger manifests. Only a few lists have been located in the National Archives of Canada, 395 Wellington Street, Ottawa, Ontario and those that do survive tend to relate mostly to immigrants from the British Isles to Quebec and Ontario between the years 1801 and 1849.

Most inwards passenger lists survive for the period 1865 until 1935 and they contain information such as name, age, country of origin, occupation and intended destination of passengers. From 1925 the lists contain additional information, including the immigrant's place of birth, the name and address of the relative, friend or employer to whom they were destined and the name and address of the nearest relative in the country from whence they came.

The records are arranged by port and date of arrival. Arrivals at Montreal tend to be included with the returns for Quebec City. Some ports do not have lists for the nineteenth century. These include Saint John, New Brunswick (from 1900); North Sydney, Nova Scotia (from 1906); Vancouver, British Columbia, and Victoria, British Columbia (both from 1905).

A series of old nominal indexes exists for the 1925 to 1935 inwards passenger lists. In co-operation with the National Archives of Canada, the Pier 21 Society in Halifax, Nova Scotia, has input the information from the passenger list indexes into a database and this is available via the National Archives of Canada web site at www.archives.ca.

### 1.4.4 USA

For the USA, as there was no legal requirement before 1820 for captains or masters of vessels to present a passenger list to US officials, few inward lists survive before this time. In 1819, the Federal Government passed legislation to monitor and check immigration and starting in 1820, Customs Passenger Lists were prepared by the ship's captain and were filed with the collector of customs at the port of arrival. It is estimated that about 90 per cent of these passenger lists have survived and have been microfilmed by the National Archives and Records Administration (NARA), 700 Pennsylvania Avenue, NW Washington, DC 20408, USA. These are also available via NARA and many State Archives and State Libraries in the USA. Further information is available via the NARA web site at www.nara.gov. Usually the following information is contained in these records: country, or town of origin, date of arrival, destination in the USA, occupation, age and gender. Many of the passenger lists have been indexed though there are important periods where no indexes exist, such as for New York from 1847 to 1897, and for Boston for 1820 to 1847 and again from 1892 to 1901. For such instances, the records are arranged chronologically and by port of arrival.

The Immigration Passenger Lists, which generally start after 1891 and supersede the Customer Passenger Lists when the Superintendent of Immigration was established in the USA, contain more information. Details available include marital status, occupation, last residence, and if going to join a relative, the relative's name, address and relationship, if in the USA before (if so, when and where), and (from 1903) the race of the passenger, physical description and birthplace. Again, the records are arranged chronologically and by state of arrival. Arrival states and ports include Alabama, Florida, Georgia, South Carolina, Baltimore, Boston, Detroit, Gloucester, New Orleans, New York, Philadelphia, Portland, Providence, San Francisco, and Seattle. Some name indexes are in the process of being made available.

One that has been completed is the Ellis Island project. Between 1892 and 1924 over 22 million passengers and members of ships' crews came through Ellis Island and the Port of New York. The American Family History Immigration Center have put these passenger lists on line at www.ellisisland.org, allowing researchers to search by name of passenger and see the original manifests too.

Many of the incoming American passenger lists have been microfilmed by the Church of Jesus Christ of Latter Day Saints (LDS) which has published a Mormons' Immigration Index on CD-ROM. Released in July 2000, this is an index to people who were passengers on LDS voyages to the US between 1840 and 1890. The majority of entries relate to British persons emigrating to the USA from the port of Liverpool to New York. Information recorded includes personal accounts of passengers for each voyage. Approximately 4,750 persons in Mormon groups left England during the period 1840–46, though many had travelled with the Mormons simply because it was a cheap and satisfactory means of travelling. Sources used to compile the data include European emigration card indexes, European mission registers, LDS publications and US customs lists. These records are explained more fully in the LDS Family Search website at www.familysearch.org.

### 1.4.5 South Africa

The first European settlement of South Africa was Cape Colony (also known as Cape Province) in 1652. Other South African provinces developed later, such as Natal, Orange Free State and Transvaal. Most South African records are kept in archives within the provinces.

Incoming Passenger Lists can be found via the Chief of the Cape Archives Repository, Private Bag X9025, Cape Town, 8000, South Africa, which include those for settlers arriving in the Cape Colony, and via the Chief of the Pietermaritzburg Archives Repository, Private Bag X9012, Pietermaritzburg, 3200, South Africa, for those settling in Natal.

## 1.5 Passport records

Passports were not compulsory for travel overseas until 1915. Before the First World War it was rare for someone travelling abroad to apply for a passport. The monarch had, until the seventeenth century, the right to control the movement of his subjects overseas, and records of applications for and grants of permission to leave the kingdom are to be found among the records of Chancery (C) and the Exchequer (E). During the eighteenth and nineteenth centuries, passports were issued more frequently, although it was only in the mid-nineteenth century that regulations relating to applications for passports were first formulated. Prior to 1858 passports could be issued to people of all nationalities whereas from 1858 the UK passport became available to UK nationals only, issued for a single journey and could be used for any subsequent journey only if countersigned afresh by the ministers or consuls of the countries which the holder intended to visit. Possession of a passport, however, was confined largely to merchants and diplomats, and the vast majority of those travelling overseas had no formal document.

Information held in the Public Record Office on individual passport-holders is scanty; the Office does not hold completed application forms, except for a small sample illustrating the treatment accorded to applications of various types.

### 1.5.1 Licences to Pass Beyond the Seas (E 157)

The records in this series consist of two main types: first, registers of people taking oaths of allegiance before leaving the realm, and second, registers of licences to pass beyond the seas. The earliest records in this class date from 1573, although regulation of travel existed before this time. The bulk of the registers come from 1613–35, with an odd one from 1677. From 1610, all people over the age of 18 travelling abroad were required to take an oath of allegiance, according to the statute 7 James I, c.6. From 1637 no passengers could go to the American colonies without a licence from the Commissioners for Plantations.

Rather surprisingly, the series includes odd registers of people travelling to Ireland and Scotland (E 157/17, 24 and 31). The bulk of the registers contain details of soldiers taking the oath of allegiance before going to serve in the Low Countries between 1613 and 1633. Some also include other persons going to continental Europe, chiefly to Holland, between 1573 and 1677.

The entries in the registers generally include date, name and destination. Age and place of residence is sometimes also recorded.

Also included in this series are several registers of passengers travelling from a number of UK ports to New England, Barbados and other colonies for 1634–9, with one of 1677. These particular registers have been printed in J C Hotten *Original Lists of Persons Emigrating to America* , *1600–1700* (London, 1874), P W Coldham *The Complete Book of Emigrants, 1607–1776*  (4 vols, Baltimore, 1987–1993) and P W Filby and M K Meyer (eds) *Passenger and Immigration Lists Index* (Detroit, 1981 and annual supplements).

**Figure 8** Licences to pass beyond the seas, 17 June 1635: passengers to be transported to New England (E 157/20 fol. 38)

### 1.5.2 Entry Books of Passes and Passport Registers

SP 25: State Papers: Books and Accounts, includes passes and warrants to go abroad. SP 25/111–116 in particular consist of passes, mainly for Europe for 1650–60. Entry Books of passes issued by the Secretaries of State between 1674 and 1784 are in the State Papers, SP 44/334–413. A further entry book of passes, some signed by the King, between 1748 and 1794 is FO 366/544. Earlier entries usually give an abstract or copy of the pass, but from January 1793 there is merely a name and a date. There is no index.

SP 44: State Papers: Entry Books: Warrants and Passes, 1661–1828, includes, in SP 44/386–413, passes for aliens going abroad and for merchants to trade overseas, giving details such as name of ship, burden, master, cargo, ports of departure and destination, and period of validity, 1697–1784. The records are indexed to 1722 and described in *Calendar of Home Office Papers in the reign of George III, 1760–1775*, available in the Map and Large Document Room. These passes were issued to prevent the return from the Continent of persons under attainder for the plot against William III in 1696.

Passport registers from 1795 to 1948 are in FO 610. The entries are chronological and show merely the date, the number of the passport issued and the name of the applicant. Early registers also show where the applicant was going and by whom he was recommended. A fresh series was started on the appointment of each new Foreign Secretary. For March to May 1915 the register is FO 613/2.

Registers of passports to Peking, China, 1874–1926, can be found in FO 563 and FO 564; to Germany, 1850–1881 in FO 155; to Hanover, 1857–1866, in FO 159/28 and 56; to Saxony and Saxon, 1819–1875, in FO 218; to Sicily and Naples, Italy, 1811–1860, in FO 166; to Mexico, 1816–1927, in FO 207; to Warsaw, Poland, 1830–1914, in FO 394, and to Barcelona, Spain, 1775–1922, in FO 639. Also, *see* 5.2.2.

### 1.5.3 Passport Indexes

Indexes of names of passport applicants are in FO 611. These cover the years 1851–62 and 1874–1916. For the latter period the index is not strictly alphabetical. There is a section of index, called a cut for each letter of the alphabet. Within the cut the names are listed chronologically. The indexes record solely the name, the number of the passport and the date of issue. The UK Passport Office, Discharge of Information Section, Aragon Court, Peterborough PE1 1QG provides a paid search service among its records of passports issued since 1898. They provide non-genealogical searches among these records and information provided includes passport number, date and place of issue, full name of bearer, place and date of birth. Searches can only be made for or with the consent of the passport-holder concerned or next of kin. The UK Passport Office also holds records of passport applications from 1990 which include address of applicant. Again, restrictions on access to these records apply.

### 1.5.4 Correspondence

Volumes of the correspondence of the Passport Office were kept in rough chronological order from 1815 to 1905 (FO 612/1–71). There is no subject index. From 1906 representative subject files are preserved, illustrating the work of the Office.

Reference to such files from 1906 to 1920 is by means of the Foreign Office card index in the Research Enquiries Room; the files selected for permanent preservation are mostly among the records of the Treaty Department (FO 372). From 1921 such files are to be found in FO 612/72–267. There are registers of correspondence for the years 1868–93 and 1898–1905 (FO 613/1–4). Two volumes of correspondence relating to the issuing of passports by British embassies and consulates and dating from 1886 and 1897–1900, respectively, are in FO 614/1–2.

### 1.5.5 Representative Case Papers

A small selection of papers illustrating the treatment accorded to applications for various types of passports, visas and certificates, dating from 1920, is preserved in FO 737/1–109. However, the 30–year closure rule applies for these records. Colonial applications for passports, 1796–1818, can be found in CO 323/97–116, and thereafter among the Original Correspondence of the colony of issue.

### 1.5.6 Representative examples of passports issued

A highly miscellaneous sample of passports is kept in FO 655. It includes some passports issued in the late eighteenth and early nineteenth centuries by foreign missions in Great Britain to British subjects wishing to travel abroad. This practice ceased in 1858. There is also a large selection of passports issued from British embassies, consulates and high commissions. There are also some foreign passports which, for some reason or another (usually cases of dual nationality), have ended up in the hands of the Passport Office. The passports are listed haphazardly, giving date and place of issue. For the early accretions to the series (up to piece 1839) there is a separate index available listing the passports alphabetically by place of issue. The records show that before 1771 British passports were written in Latin or English and between 1772 and 1858 they were in French. After 1858 they have been written in English with, since 1921, French translations for certain sections. Photographs of holders have been included since 1915, when the first modern passport was issued after the enactment of the 1914 British Nationality and Status of Aliens Act (4 & 5 Geo. V c.17). From 1915 until 1923 UK passports were valid for two years but could be renewed for a further four two-year periods. From 1924 until 1967 passports were issued for five years with a renewal period of five years. The standard 10-year passports were introduced in 1968.

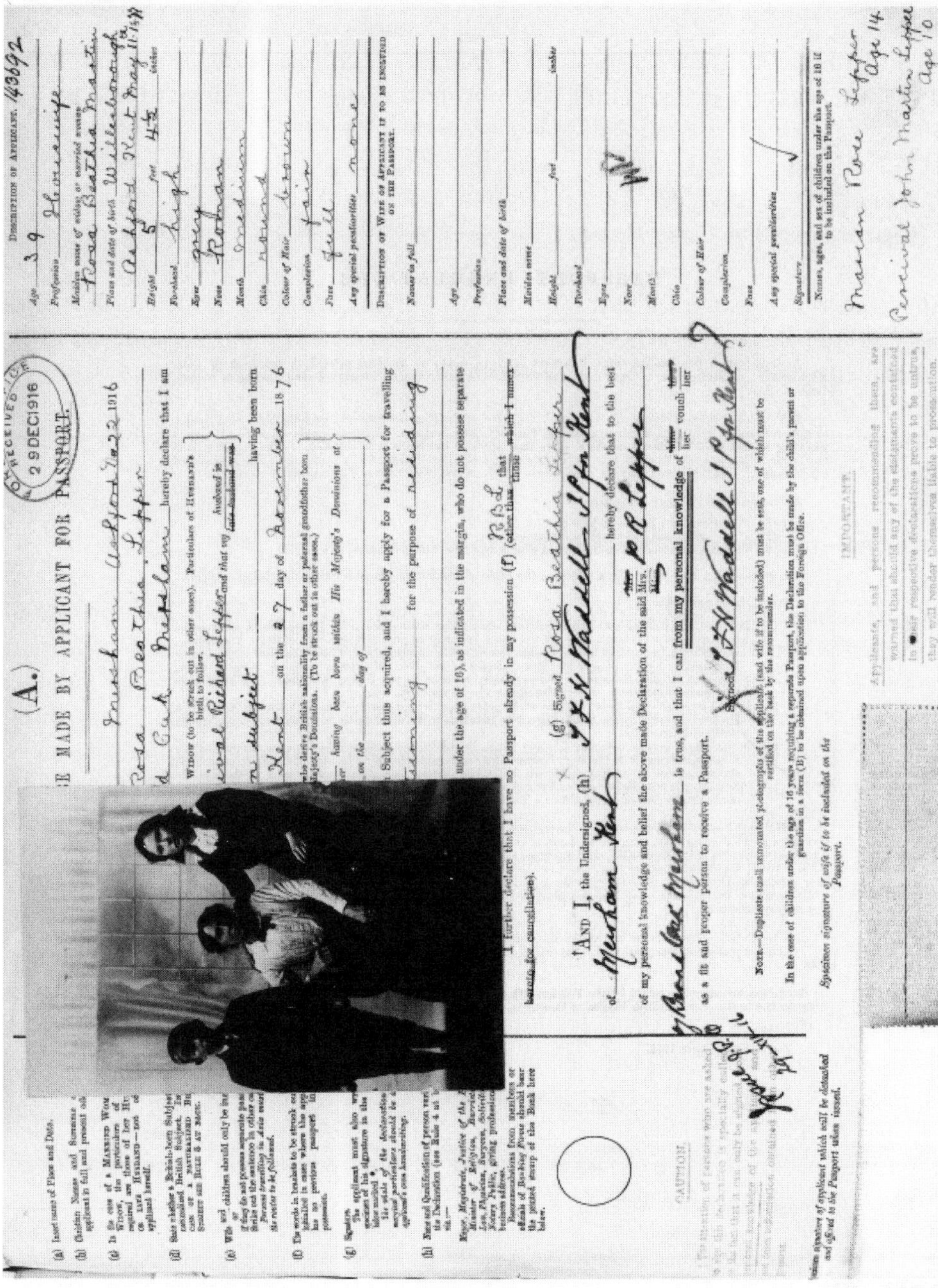

**Figure 9** Application for Passport by Rosa Beathia Lepper and her children Marian Rose (14) and John Martin (10) for travel to Canada, 22 December 1916 (FO 737/24)

## 1.5.7 Colonial passports

The Colonial Office was responsible for issuing passports to people going to the colonies.

CO 323: Colonies General, includes applications for passports to the colonies, 1796–1818 in CO 323/97–116. After 1818, applications for passports to the colonies are bound with the ordinary correspondence series for the relevant colony, until responsibility for passports to all destinations passed to the Foreign Office in 1916.

# 2 Emigration to the Colonies and Dominions

Europe has always had a mobile population, and with the discovery of the Americas, and the opening up of trade routes to the sub-Sahara Africa and the Orient, many people seized the opportunity to seek for wealth. People rapidly emigrated and populated the New World because of the new sources of revenue, the chance to expand boundaries and to get rid of undesirables. The early colonists were merchants, adventurers (pirates, buccaneers, etc.) and pioneers. But it was not too long before many were forced to settle, such as rebels, prisoners and bonded labourers.

Colonial population was not static. For example, after the American War of Independence, Loyalists left for Canada, Nova Scotia, the Bahamas and England. Also, after the abolition of slavery, emigrants from the Indian sub-continent were encouraged to emigrate to the West Indies to help with local labour problems, as indentured/bonded labour.

In terms of the scale of emigration, it is clear that emigration to the colonies was widespread from the seventeenth century. It is estimated that around 1.7 million people left the UK during the seventeenth and eighteenth centuries with a further 10 million during the nineteenth and twentieth centuries.

Sources relating to involuntary emigrants (mainly transportees) are discussed in Chapter 4. Although there are very many references in documents in the Public Record Office to individuals and families voluntarily emigrating to various colonies, there is no single index to the names of such persons. As this chapter will show, the chief sources of information are in the numerous series of Colonial Office (CO) records and Dominion Office (DO) records and in a few series of Privy Council (PC), Treasury (T) and Audit Office (AO) records.

Common sources relating to emigration to general destinations such as passenger lists are discussed in Chapter 1. Similarly, Chapter 5 looks at general life-cycle sources for emigrants in all recipient areas. This chapter looks specifically at emigration to the colonies and those records relating to emigration schemes and voluntary settlement there. Dealt with separately, in Chapter 3, are child migration schemes.

## 2.1 Emigration to all colonies and dominions – general sources

### 2.1.1 Printed sources

Much of the information relating to emigration to the colonies has been printed in some form. Most of it is administrative in character, but it can include useful genealogical material. Main published sources include the records of the Privy Council (PC 1, 2 and 5), printed as *Acts of the Privy Council of England, Colonial Series.* Various useful classes of Treasury papers, registers and indexes including T 1, 2, 3 and 4, and T 108, contain considerable reference to Colonial Office business. Many of these have been described and indexed in the *Calendar of Treasury Papers, 1557–1728, Calendar of Treasury Books, 1660–1718,* and the *Calendar of Treasury Books and Papers, 1729–1745* and include reference to other Treasury series, such as T 7: Treasury: Books of Out-letters concerning Colonial Affairs, 1849–1921; T 27: General Out-letter Books, 1668–1920; T 28: Treasury: Various Out-letter Books, 1763–1885; T 29: Minute Books, 1667–1870; T 38: Treasury: Departmental Accounts, 1558–1937; and T 99: Minute Books, Supplementary, 1690–1832; T 52: Entry Books of Royal Warrants, 1667–1857; T 53: Entry Books of Royal Warrants Relating to the Payment of Money, 1676–1839; T 54: Entry Books of Warrants concerning Appointments, Crown Leases and other, 1667 to 1849; and T 60: Order Books, 1667–1831.

Many senior civil servants who were posted for service overseas or in the colonies are best sought, not in the records, but in such publications as the *Dictionary of National Biography,* or the *British Biographical Archive.* There are a number of official printed sources available at Kew on the postings of senior civil servants, but they do not provide personal information. The main one is the *British Imperial Calendar,* which runs from 1810 to 1972, when it became the *Civil Service Year Book.* From 1852 there is the *Foreign Office List,* and from 1862 the *Colonial Office List.* The *Diplomatic Service List* runs from 1966, and the *Commonwealth Relations Office List* from 1953. All are on open access in the Research Enquiries Room. There is also, available in the Library, the useful source David P Henige, *Colonial Governors from the fifteenth century to the present: a comprehensive list* (University of Wisconsin, Madison, 1970),

### 2.1.2 Colonial Office and Foreign Office records

The records of the Colonial Office include much material relating to emigrants to all colonies. CO 384: Emigration Original Correspondence, 1817–1896 contains many letters from settlers or people intending to settle in British North America, Australia, the West Indies and other places: there are separate registers for British North America (*see* 2.2). Details of land grants and applications may be found in CO 323: Colonies, General: Original Correspondence, 1689–1952; CO 324: Colonies, General:

**Figure 10**  Barbados, Government Gazette, 29 April 1867: includes marriage and death returns (CO 32/1A)

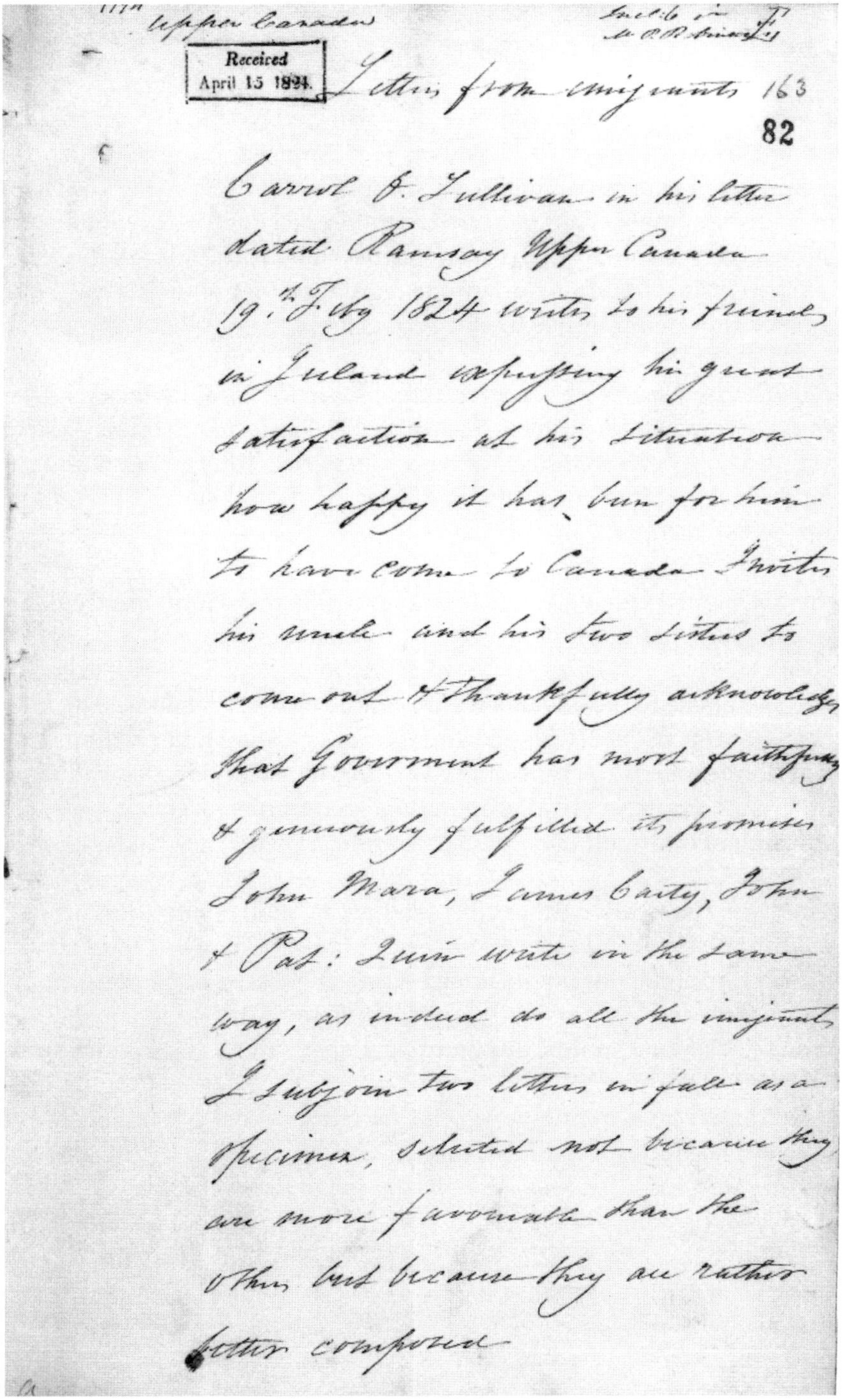

Received
April 15 1824.

Letter from emigrants 163

82

Carrol O. Sullivan in his letter dated Ramsay Upper Canada 19th Feby 1824 writes to his friends in Ireland expressing his great satisfaction at his situation how happy it has been for him to have come to Canada Invites his uncle and his two sisters to come out & thankfully acknowledges that Government has most faithfully & generously fulfilled its promises John Mara, James Carty, John & Pat: Quin write in the same way, as indeed do all the emigrants I subjoin two letters in full as a specimen, selected not because they are more favourable than the others but because they are rather better composed

**Figure 11** Letter from emigrant Carrol Sullivan, 1824 (CO 384/12, fol. 82)

Entry Books Series I, 1662–1872; and CO 381: Colonies, General: Entry Books Series II, 1835–1872.

The Land and Emigration Commission was established in 1833 to promote emigration by providing free passage and land grants. The Emigration Entry Books, 1814–1871 (CO 385) and the Land and Emigration Commission Papers, 1833–1894 (CO 386) give names of emigrants. CO 386 also contains records of the South Australian Colonization Commission, a predecessor of the Land and Emigration Commission, which was responsible for laying down the regulations for land sales and overseeing the selection of emigrants eligible for a free passage.

CO 386/29 details the government regulations set for local agents when selecting emigrants for free passages to New South Wales, Western Australia, Tasmania and New Zealand. The criteria for selection were very strict. You can often find references to payments which covered emigrants' travel expenses to their port of embarkation in locally kept parish records.

Other general Colonial Office sources for emigrants include individual colony's entry books, government gazettes, blue books and colonial newspapers.

Entry books (available to the late nineteenth century for most colonies) include details of patents and grants of land. Colonial government gazettes and colonial newspapers are similar in style and in the type of information they provide. As well as statistical information on subjects such as population, geography and accounts, they also contain a wealth of information of interest to genealogists. These include:

- birth, marriage and death notifications (and occasionally obituaries);
- notices of proceedings and sales in the local courts of Chancery and Petty Sessions;
- lists of people applying for liquor licences, dog licences, gun licences, etc.;
- lists of jurors, constables, nurses, druggists, solicitors, etc.;
- notices of sales of land, public appointments, leave of absence and resumption of duty;
- notices relating to cases of intestacy, wills, executors, etc.;
- notices on applications for naturalization;
- inquests into wrecks;
- lists of ships entering and clearing port, often with the names of first class passengers;
- lists of people in arrears of militia tax;
- lists of people who paid parish relief.

They can also help to piece together the careers of colonial civil servants recording appointments and promotions. References to individual colony series of Government Gazettes and Colonial Newspapers can be found in the CO Index, available at the

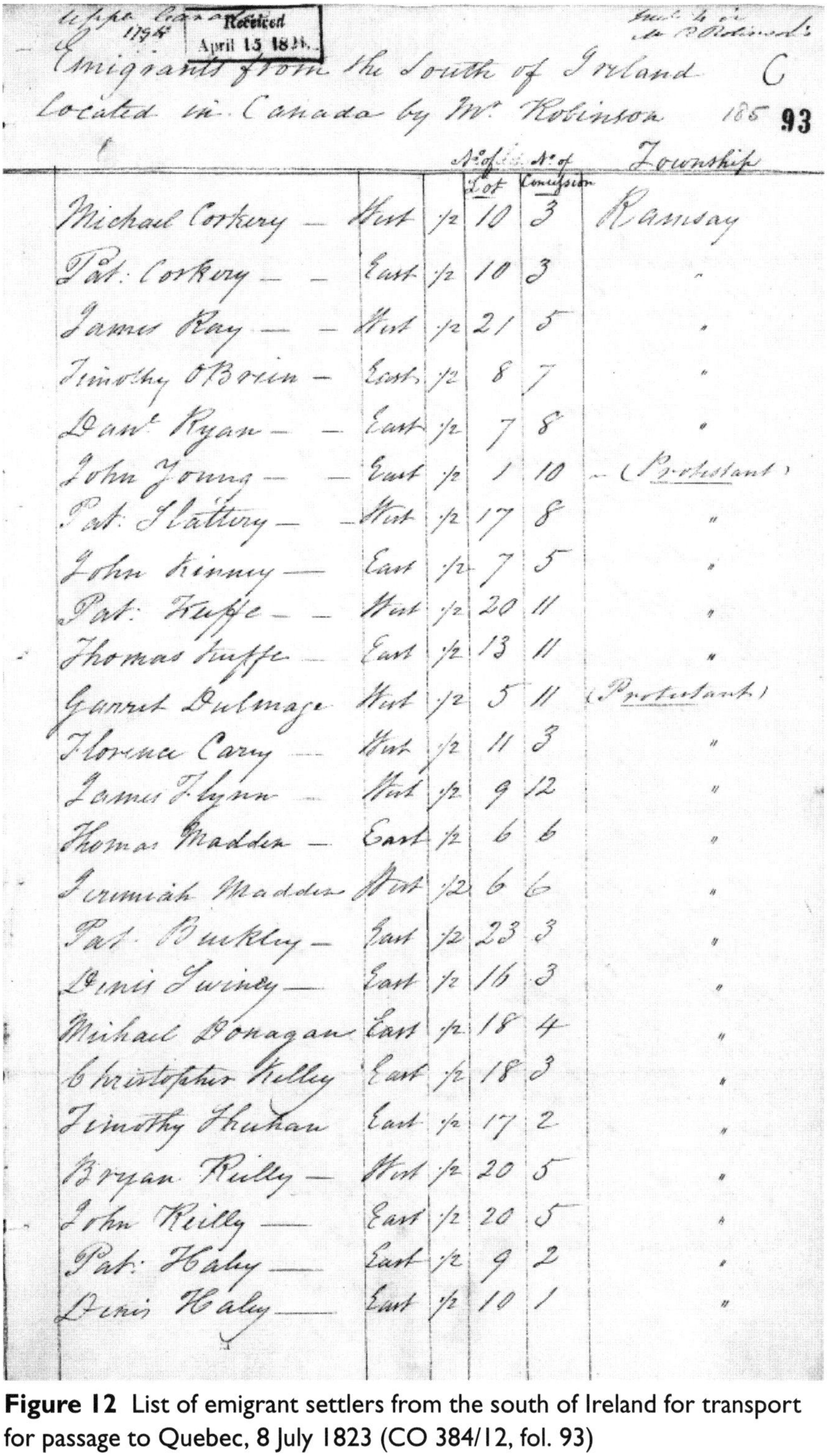

| | | | No. of Lot | No. of Concession | Township |
|---|---|---|---|---|---|
| Michael Corkery | West | 1/2 | 10 | 3 | Ramsay |
| Pat. Corkery | East | 1/2 | 10 | 3 | " |
| James Roy | West | 1/2 | 21 | 5 | " |
| Timothy oBrien | East | 1/2 | 8 | 7 | " |
| Dan Ryan | East | 1/2 | 7 | 8 | " |
| John Young | East | 1/2 | 1 | 10 | (Protestant) |
| Pat. Slattery | West | 1/2 | 17 | 8 | " |
| John Kinney | East | 1/2 | 7 | 5 | " |
| Pat. Tuffe | West | 1/2 | 20 | 11 | " |
| Thomas Tuffe | East | 1/2 | 13 | 11 | " |
| Garret Dulmage | West | 1/2 | 5 | 11 | (Protestant) |
| Florence Carey | West | 1/2 | 11 | 3 | " |
| James Flynn | West | 1/2 | 9 | 12 | " |
| Thomas Madden | East | 1/2 | 6 | 6 | " |
| Jeremiah Madden | West | 1/2 | 6 | 6 | " |
| Pat. Buckley | East | 1/2 | 23 | 3 | " |
| Denis Swiney | East | 1/2 | 16 | 3 | " |
| Michael Donagan | East | 1/2 | 18 | 4 | " |
| Christopher Kelly | East | 1/2 | 18 | 3 | " |
| Timothy Sheehan | East | 1/2 | 17 | 2 | " |
| Bryan Reilly | West | 1/2 | 20 | 5 | " |
| John Reilly | East | 1/2 | 20 | 5 | " |
| Pat. Haley | East | 1/2 | 9 | 2 | " |
| Denis Haley | East | 1/2 | 10 | 1 | " |

Emigrants from the South of Ireland Located in Canada by Mr. Robinson 1823

**Figure 12** List of emigrant settlers from the south of Ireland for transport for passage to Quebec, 8 July 1823 (CO 384/12, fol. 93)

Research Enquiries Desk and also in A Thurston, *Records of the Colonial Office, Dominions Office, Commonwealth Relations Office and Commonwealth Office* (London, 1995). The British Library Newspaper Library, Colindale Avenue, London NW9 5HE also holds an excellent collection of colonial newspapers and early gazettes.

The indexes to general correspondence of the Foreign Office (FO) can also contain useful information relating to emigrants and expatriates. The general correspondence consists of the original papers accumulated in London, that is the original dispatches from British representatives abroad with any enclosures; drafts of outgoing dispatches; minutes; domestic correspondence with foreign representatives in this country, with other branches of the British government and with private individuals and bodies.

Records earlier in date than 1906 are to be found in the series FO 1–FO 84, FO 90–FO 92, and FO 95–FO 111. For the most part, they are arranged by country. In addition, there are some series of a general or miscellaneous nature not related to a particular country. Departmental diaries and registers, and general registers 1817–1920, are in the series Registers of General Correspondence (FO 566), and for the most part record the arrival and handling of individual papers and dispatch of replies. Each register for each country has an index and copies of these are available on microfilm in FO 605.

Indexes for the period 1906 to 1919 is covered by a card index in the Research Enquiries Room. From 1920 to 1951 the index is in the form of printed volumes, also held here, and for the years 1952, 1953 and 1959 there are similar non-published departmental indexes also held in the research enquiries room. These indexes mainly refer to papers in FO 371: Political Departments but some refer to other departments such as FO 369: Consular Department, FO 370: Library and Research Departments, FO 372: Treaty Department and FO 395: News Department. For the years 1954 to 1958 and from 1960 to 1966 there are no detailed indexes in these classes and it is necessary to consult the relevant class lists to access the records. From 1967 to October 1968, when the Foreign and Commonwealth Office was formed, the political departments of the Foreign Office operated a common registry system with the Commonwealth Office and the Diplomatic Service Administration Office, and records from this period can be found in various FCO classes by department.

### 2.1.3 Soldier Resettlement records

During the nineteenth century, army pensioners were encouraged to settle in British colonies, although many of them failed as settlers. References to the settlement of ex-soldiers in Australia and New Zealand will be found in the PRO's *Alphabetical Guide to Certain War Office and Other Military Records (List and Index volume 53)*, under the name of the relevant colony.

WO 43: War Office: Secretary-at-War, Correspondence, Very Old Series (VOS) and Old Series (OS), 1809–1857, contains papers relating to particular emigrant officers and soldiers in relation to half-pay, pensions, annuities and allowances. Similarly, references to former soldiers who settled in any colony can be found in WO 22: Royal Hospital Chelsea: Pensions Returns, 1842–1883. This series consists of periodical returns of pensions paid or payable by the Royal Hospital Chelsea, bound up in volumes and arranged under the various districts in the United Kingdom, Channel Islands, etc., and in India, the Colonies and certain foreign stations. They include returns of out-pensioners of Chelsea and Greenwich Hospitals, of those belonging to the East India Company, and of mercantile marine pensioners; also annual mortality returns showing the number of deaths at different ages. In addition to the statistical information which these returns supply they are useful for tracing changes of residence and dates of death of individual pensioners.

The first official to promote soldier resettlement during the First World War was William Ferguson Massey, Prime Minister of New Zealand, 1912–1925. He visualized the settlement of 'patriot soldiers' across the Empire. New Zealand legislated to encourage immigration, as did all the Dominions by 1918.

Unofficial bodies had been pressing for resettlement since before the war. The Royal Colonial Institution (RCI) was prominent and it was largely RCI pressure which led to imperial migration being discussed at the 1911 Imperial Conference.

Demobilization in 1918 resulted in the 1922 Empire Settlement Act, with free passages to the Dominions. Some 40,000 ex-soldiers emigrated, mostly to Canada. The resettlement schemes were generally considered to be a failure. Those who took the option were too few, and the world industrial slump of the 1920s left them in an exposed position. Many lacked the determination and skills to work on the land in hard times. They suffered financial ruin in their thousands, leaving Dominion governments to carry the debts. Leaving the land, they became a new unemployed urban class in the Dominions' major towns and cities. The only plus was the development of virgin land – few of the political objectives were achieved.

The soldier resettlement policy for this period largely resulted in the formation of the Overseas Settlement Committee, which was eventually taken over by the Overseas Settlement Board in 1925, *see* 2.1.5.

Archive sources, including case studies, are available mainly at the archives of the receiving countries. PRO record series relating to policy include CO 721: Overseas Settlement Department: Original Correspondence, 1918–1925; and CO 532: Dominions Original Correspondence, 1907–1925. Relevant specific pieces include CAB 27/174: Overseas Settlement, 1922; and CAB 37/144/75: Report of the Cabinet Committee on Land Settlement for Sailors and Soldiers, 1916.

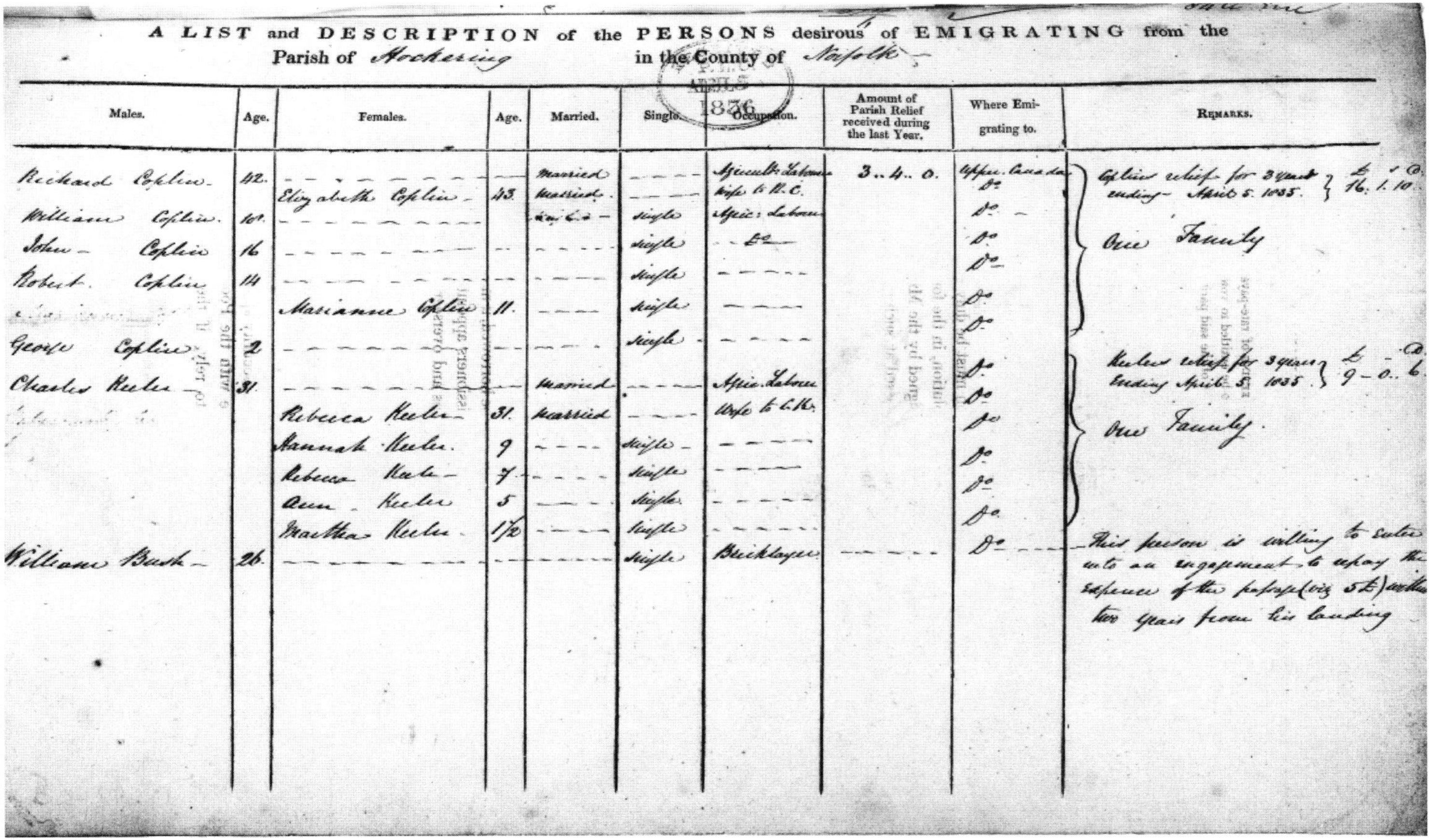

A LIST and DESCRIPTION of the PERSONS desirous of EMIGRATING from the Parish of Hockering in the County of Norfolk

| Males. | Age. | Females. | Age. | Married. | Single. | Occupation. | Amount of Parish Relief received during the last Year. | Where Emigrating to. | Remarks. |
|---|---|---|---|---|---|---|---|---|---|
| Richard Coplin | 42 | | | married | | Agricult. Labourer | 3..4..0 | Upper Canada | Coplin relief for 3 years ending April 5. 1835 } £16. 1. 10 |
| | | Elizabeth Coplin | 43 | married | | Wife to R.C. | | Do | |
| William Coplin | 10 | | | | single | Agric. Labourer | | Do | One Family |
| John Coplin | 16 | | | | single | Do | | Do | |
| Robert Coplin | 14 | | | | single | | | Do | |
| | | Marianne Coplin | 11 | | single | | | Do | |
| George Coplin | 2 | | | | single | | | Do | |
| Charles Keeler | 31 | | | married | | Agric. Labourer | | Do | Keeler relief for 3 years ending April 5. 1835 } £9 - 0 - 6 |
| | | Rebecca Keeler | 31 | married | | Wife to C.K. | | Do | One Family |
| | | Hannah Keeler | 9 | | single | | | Do | |
| | | Rebecca Keeler | 7 | | single | | | Do | |
| | | Ann Keeler | 5 | | single | | | Do | |
| | | Martha Keeler | 1½ | | single | | | Do | |
| William Bush | 26 | | | | single | Bricklayer | | Do | This person is willing to enter into an engagement to repay the expence of the passage (viz 5£) within two years from his landing |

**Figure 13** List of persons intending to emigrate from the parish of Hockering, Norfolk (MH 12/8474)

Many British troops already stationed in America during the nineteenth century applied for land grants; *see* 2.2.3 for further information.

### 2.1.4 Poor Law records

Many poor emigrants were provided with assistance for the passage by their parish, under the provisions of the 1834 Poor Law Amendment Act. The records of the administration of this assistance (MH 12) can include lists of emigrants, giving their occupation and destination: however, they are very voluminous, are arranged chronologically by county and Poor Law Union, not by subject, so details can be very difficult to find. Similar records relating to parish-organized emigration will be found locally at appropriate County Record Offices.

MH 19: Local Government Board and predecessors: Correspondence with Government Offices, 1834–1909, contains correspondence of the Poor Law Commission and Board and the Local Government Board with other government departments, the Metropolitan Police, the Metropolitan Board of Works and parliamentary officers relating to poor law administration and, after 1871, public health and local government services.

The series includes volumes of internal correspondence and papers of the Poor Law Board and the Local Government Board, including draft orders and Bills, minutes and memoranda on establishment and organization matters, precedents, general questions of administration and correspondence with the Treasury. Some volumes relate to specific subjects, particularly plague, but also anthrax, cholera, leprosy, smallpox, yellow fever, quarantine and emigration. The records are arranged by names of corresponding departments. Registers of correspondence are in MH 20. MH 19/22 relates specifically to passage assisted emigration and includes lists of emigrant ships reported to have arrived in British territories between 1836 and 1876.

### 2.1.5 Overseas Settlement Board

In 1925, the Overseas Settlement Department and the Overseas Settlement Committee were transferred from the Colonial Office to the Dominions Office. An inter-Departmental Committee on Migration Policy examined the whole question of emigration from the United Kingdom to the Commonwealth, and recommended (Cmd 4689 of 1934) a revised system. In 1936 the department ceased to exist as a separate entity and the committee was replaced by the Overseas Settlement Board, responsible for advising the secretary of state on matters of migration policy. The Board was composed of five non-official members appointed by the Secretary of State, to represent respectively organized labour, business interests, social services, women's interests and migration organization; three officials from the Treasury and the Dominions Office; and was chaired by the Parliamentary Under Secretary for Dominions Affairs. The Board was purely advisory in function, unlike the earlier Committee, as the reduced number of emigrants meant that there was no justification for an extensive government service to migrants, and it did not take on the functions of interviewing candidates and publishing information and advice that the Committee had exercised. Its activities were suspended at the outbreak of the Second World War, which it did not survive.

Under the Commonwealth Relations Office (CRO), the Board was revived with the same terms of reference in the form of the Overseas Migration Board in 1953, as the numbers of emigrants increased to pre-1930 levels. In the new Board, the official members were replaced by three members of parliament, and the joint secretaries were from the CRO and the Ministry of Labour. Officials from both these departments attended Board meetings as observers.

Correspondence of the Overseas Settlement Department is in DO 57, with registers in DO 5 and DO 6. Minutes of the meetings of the Overseas Settlement Board are in DO 114/89–90. The papers of W B Amery while British government representative in Australia for migration (1925–8) and principal, Overseas Settlement Department (1929–31) are in DO 190. Records of the CRO departments that dealt with the Overseas Migration Board are in the MIG series in DO 35 and DO 175.

### 2.1.6 Registration of British citizenship overseas

Between 1740 and 1773 foreign Protestants in the Americas could also be naturalized as British by the taking of oaths in court and lists of those naturalized may be found in CO 5 and in the related entry books in CO 324/55–56.

In 1696, the mayor, recorder and commonalty of New York City swore the oath of association in support of William III: the resulting oath roll contains the signatures and marks of much of the male population of the city (C 213/470).

Files on individuals who, under section 8 of the British Nationality and Status of Aliens Act 1914, were granted certificates of naturalization by governments of British Possessions overseas may be found in CO 323, CO 1032 and DO 35 and also relevant CO and DO country correspondence classes. It should be noted, however, that few individual case files survive. Duplicate Home Office certificates of such naturalizations from 1 January 1915 may be found in HO 334. Indexes to names of persons naturalized by Governors of British Possessions and references to the Home Office certificates can be found among the printed indexes to naturalizations, available in the

**Figure 14** African Department: General Correspondence: Congo Affairs. (21,864–42,821), 1912. Photograph of British missionaries in Sonabata (FO 367/316)

Research Enquiries Room. The certificates provide the following information: name, date and place of birth, marital status, address, occupation and details of parents. They include cases relating to British born women who lost their British status upon marriage to a non-British subject. Often, after being widowed, they would apply for naturalization so that they could regain their British status. Notices on applications for naturalization can also be found among colonial government gazettes and colonial newspapers (*see* 2.1.2).

### 2.1.7 Missionary records

There are a number of collections of missionary society records which may assist in the tracing of emigrants.

The Fulham Papers in the Lambeth Palace Library, London SE1 7JU (Tel: 020 7928 6222), comprise the archive of the bishops of London. The majority of the collection date from the eighteenth and nineteenth centuries and includes correspondence on the administration of the diocese of London, and on the churches, particularly in America and the West Indies, which came under the bishop's jurisdiction before the founding of the separate episcopates in those countries. The records available at the Lambeth Palace Library include ordination papers for the American and West Indies colonies, 1748–1824, lists of ministers receiving missionary bonds for the royal bounty for migration to the colonies, 1748–1811, appointments of clergy, 1718–1774, lists of clergy and public officials 1723–1748, licences for curates, preachers, lecturers, schoolmasters, and licences to officiate in the colonies.

The library also holds returns of clergy queries. Sent to all colonial clergy by Bishop Edmund Gibson in 1723, the returns of these queries present an interesting picture of colonial church life with biographical information of the clergy.

Other papers available include those relating to emigration schemes and the assistance of those emigrating from the UK, 1905–1928, Church Emigration Society papers, and an indexed calendar of the papers and correspondence of the Archbishop of Canterbury relating to Anglicans in the Antipodes, in particular emigration schemes, juvenile emigration and Empire settlement from the 1780s.

The Church Mission Society, Partnership House, 157 Waterloo Road, London SE1 8UU (Tel: 020 7928 8681; web site www.cms-uk.org), the Baptist Mission Society, Regent's Park College, Pusey Street, Oxford OX1 2LB (Tel: 01865 288142; web site www.rpc.ox. ac.uk/rpc), and the School for Oriental and African Studies, Library (Archives), Thornhaugh Street, Russell Street, London WC1H 0XG (Tel: 020 7898 4180; web site www.soas.ac.uk are also good sources for records relating to missionaries.

A major collection of School for Oriental and African Studies (SOAS) are the Missionary Archives, including those of the China Inland Missionary (now the Overseas Missionary Fellowship), 1872–1951, the Conference of British Missionary Societies, 1910–1912, the London Missionary Society (now the Council for World Mission), 1795–1970, the Melanesian Mission, *c.* 1872–1970, the Presbyterian Church of England's Foreign Missions Committee, *c.* 1900–1970.

Founded in 1799, the Church Mission Society (CMS) was established to send Christians, lay and clergy, to Africa and the East to share the Good News proclaimed by Jesus Christ. With an estimated 2 million items, the Special Collections, Main Library, University of Birmingham, Edgbaston, Birmingham B15 2TT holds by far the largest collection of CMS archives. It has been received in instalments from 1979, and papers from the Society's foundation in 1799 up to 1949 are currently open for scholarly study. The collection is a rich source of information not only for ecclesiastical history but for the secular history and anthropology of the many countries, particularly in Asia and Africa, in which the Society has operated. Included are records of the Society's home administration (minute books, ledgers, correspondence and publications) and of the work of individual missions, amongst them letters and diaries kept by missionaries. Over the years the Society has absorbed three other missionary societies, and their archives too now form part of the collection in the University Library; they are the Church of England Zenana Missionary Society (founded 1880), the Female Education Society (founded 1834) and the Loochoo Naval Mission (founded 1843).

The Baptist Missionary Society (BMS), founded by William Carey when he set out for India in 1793, has deposited its archives at Regent's Park College, Oxford. The archives there include missionary correspondence.

## 2.2 Emigration to North America and the West Indies – special sources

British colonies were established in North America from 1607, and during the course of the seventeenth century a succession of committees, commissions and councils of trade and plantations, all to a greater or lesser degree subordinate to the Privy Council, were established to superintend the affairs of the new colonies in America and the West Indies. The last of these, the lords of trade and plantations or Board of Trade, was established in 1696 and continued until 1782. Although from 1675 the secretaries of state were always lords of trade, their involvement in colonial affairs was at first slight and only developed in the eighteenth century.

The major early collection of papers relating to the West Indies and the American colonies (CO 1) has been described and indexed in the *Calendar of State Papers, Colonial, America and West Indies,* (now available on CD-ROM), which includes references to the many other succeeding classes as well. It is also worth searching the following series of original correspondence for North America, together with its related registers in the following series: CO 5: America and West Indies, Original Correspondence, 1606–1822; CO 6: British North America Original Correspondence, 1816–1868; CO 42: Canada, formerly British North America, Original Correspondence, 1700–1922; CO 60: British Columbia, Original Correspondence, 1858–1871; CO 188: New Brunswick Original Correspondence, 1784–1867; CO 194: Newfoundland Original Correspondence, 1696–1922; CO 217: Nova Scotia and Cape Breton Original Correspondence, 1710–1867; CO 226: Prince Edward Island Original Correspondence, 1769–1873; CO 326: General Registers, 1633–1849; CO 327: British North America Emigration Registers, 1850–1863; CO 328: British North America General Registers (including emigration 1864–1868); CO 329: British North America Registers of Out-letters, 1872–1880; PC 1: Privy Council and Privy Council Office: Miscellaneous Unbound Papers, 1481–1946; PC 5: Privy Council Office: Plantation Books, 1678–1806;  SP 54: Secretaries of State: State Papers Scotland Series II, 1688–1782 (for Scottish emigrants); and T 1: Treasury: Papers, 1557–1920.

## 2.2.1 Company and Society records

### 2.2.1.1 Hudson's Bay Company

Founded in 1670, the Hudson's Bay Company's (HBC) chief interests for its first two centuries were the fur trade, exploration and settlement. After 1870, when its territory of Rupert's Land was incorporated into the Dominion of Canada, its interests became more varied.

BH 1 comprises the following eight types of records of the Hudson's Bay Company:

- Headquarters records;
- Records concerning posts in North America;
- Logs, books and papers relating to ships in the service of the company;
- Governors' papers;
- Miscellaneous records, which include correspondence and journals of various individuals, as well as records of the Red River Settlement (1811–1890), Vancouver Island colony (1848–1861), Arctic expeditions (1824–1866), and the Parliamentary select committees;
- Records of allied and subsidiary companies, which include the North West Company (1786–1851), the Puget's Sound Agricultural Company (1838–1932), the International Financial Society Ltd (1859–1869), the Russian American Company (1821–1903), the Assiniboine Wool Company (1829–1836), the Red River Tallow Company (1832–1833), the Vancouver Island Steam Sawmill Company (1852–1856), the Vancouver Coal Mining Company (1861–1900), and the Buffalo Wool Company (1822–1824);
- Western Department land records;
- Records from the Commissioner's Office in Winnipeg.

The series also includes manuscript and published maps, charts and plans of Hudson's Bay Company forts, coal mines, various American and British territories and Canadian cities and towns, together with architects' drawings, specifications and atlases.

The records in BH 1 are microfilm copies of original records held at the Hudson's Bay Company Archives (HBCA), Provincial Archives of Manitoba, 200 Vaughan Street, Winnipeg, Manitoba R3C 1T5. Access is subject to a specified undertaking (available at the PRO), as required by HBCA. Further information about these records and the history of the company can be found at the HBCA web site at www.gov.mb.ca/chc/archives/hbca/.

## 2.2.1.2 West New Jersey Society

The West New Jersey Society was a company formed about 1691 for the development of the 'Hereditary Government of West Jersey in America'. Tracts of land in West and East New Jersey, Pennsylvania, New England and elsewhere were divided into 1,600 parts, forming the shares of the adventurers. These on death fell to the heirs, executors or administrators of the deceased.

The affairs of the Society failed to prosper and by the turn of the seventeenth century its development work had practically ended, although it remained possessed of its lands and property. These were gradually disposed of and by 1819 the whole of the Society's assets had been realized. Thereafter, its duties consisted of dividing its assets among its shareholders.

In 1914 only twenty-eight and one third shares remained unclaimed, and in November of that year a Statement of Claim (Hovell and others v Attorney General 1914 H No 2476) was filed by three persons representing the Society, in which they stated their readiness to deal with the funds constituting the remaining shares, if still unclaimed, as *bona vacantia* belonging to the Crown. These funds were transferred to the Crown, by an order in Chancery of March 1923.

Records of the West New Jersey Society consisting of original in-letters, entry books and drafts of out-letters, minute books of its court and committees, ledgers and accounts, registers of the transfer of shares, maps and plans, original deeds and charters, a history of the society, and miscellaneous papers relating to claims, etc., of legal and historical importance can be found in TS 12. The records date from 1658–1921. Although the records throw little light upon the Society's trading activities during the early years of its existence, they provide much information concerning its holdings of land in New Jersey. Details concerning the management and disposal of these can be obtained from the Society's correspondence with its agents in America as well as from its minute and letter books, accounts, deeds, plans, etc. The records, and particularly the accounts and share registers, also illustrate the gradual distribution of the Society's assets among those persons with a claim on its shares. A significant gap is the absence of a minute book for the period between 1703 and 1728. However, it is suggested in the Society's official history that this might be because little business of note was transacted during that time.

## 2.2.2 American Loyalist Claims and Florida Claims

The peace treaty signed at the end of the American War of Independence in 1783 provided for a recommendation by the Congress of the United States for the restoration of the property of 'real British subjects'.

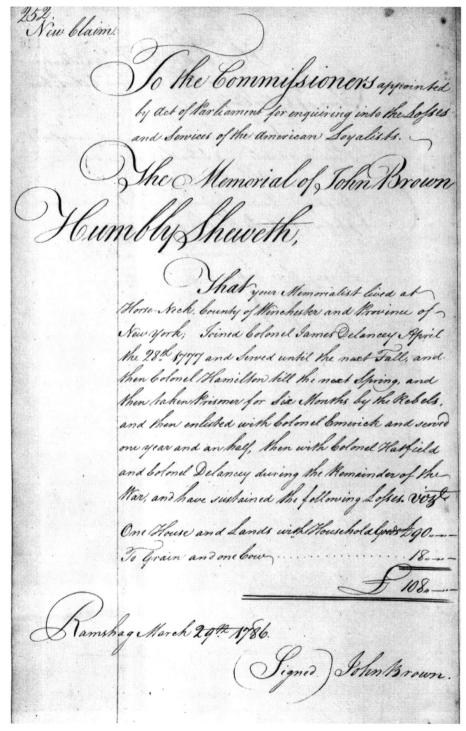

**Figure 15**  Claim of John Brown, late of New York, October 1786 (AO 12/23)

This recommendation was intended to cover the claims of those Americans who had suffered losses during the war as a result of their loyalty to the Crown but it soon became apparent that they could expect little redress from the legislatures of individual states. In fact, British commissioners had already been appointed under the American Loyalists' Act 1783 to inquire into the losses of such persons and many of them were awarded pensions and compensations by the British government.

Claims in respect of debts were, however, excluded as the 1783 peace treaty provided that creditors on either side should meet no lawful impediment in seeking to recover debts due to them. In practice, there were many difficulties particularly as, in the case of loyalist claimants, their attainder was invariably held by the American courts to bar their suit.

In 1794 a new treaty, commonly known as Jay's Treaty, was signed between Great Britain and the United States. The sixth article of this treaty provided for the settlement of all debts contracted with and due to British subjects prior to the peace of 1783. A seventh article provided for the payment of claims for compensation for losses and damages suffered by American merchants and citizens during the war by reason of irregular or illegal captures of vessels and property. Two boards of commissioners were established to carry these articles into effect. Each consisted of two British and two American commissioners with a fifth appointed by the other four. In 1799, deadlock having arisen in the settlement of claims under the sixth article, the British government, as a counter-measure, suspended its proceedings under the seventh article.

In 1802 a new convention was signed by the two countries for the mutual payment of claims. The board constituted under the seventh article of the treaty of 1794 resumed its work and the American government undertook to pay the sum of £600,000 in satisfaction of the money they might otherwise have been liable to pay under the terms of the sixth article.

To deal with claims under this article in respect of outstanding debts from British merchants and from Americans who had remained loyal to the Crown, three commissioners were appointed in Britain under the Distribution of Certain Monies Act 1803. Two of these commissioners had previously represented Great Britain on the former board established for this purpose under the 1794 treaty, while the third had sat on that board as its fifth member, having been chosen by lot in 1797.

Claims amounting to nearly £5 million were considered by these commissioners of which £1,420,000 were allowed to be good. Successful claimants received dividends pro rata from the money made available by the American government which, with interest, amounted to £659,493. The commission made its final adjudication on claims in 1811 and presented its last report to the Treasury in June 1812 when it wound up its proceedings.

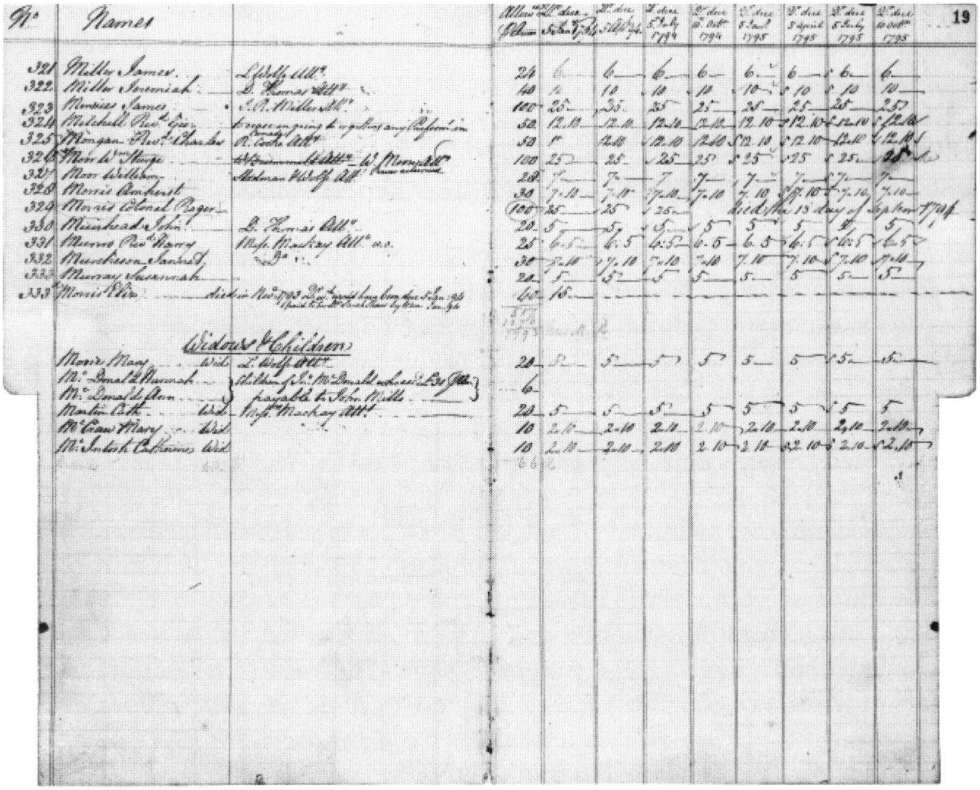

**Figure 16** Pay Lists: Refugees, 1794–5 (T50/14, p.19)

Records of the claims for compensation of American citizens who suffered property losses through loyalty to the British Crown during the war of American Independence can be found in AO 12: Audit Office: American Loyalist Claims Series I, 1776–1812; AO 13: Audit Office: American Loyalist Claims Series II, 1780–1835; and T 79: American Loyalist Claims Commission, 1777–1841.

AO 12 and AO 13 consist of entry books and ledgers containing the evidence of witnesses, reports and other communicated documents, the examinations and decisions of the commissioners, lists of claims, etc. Researchers visiting the PRO may consult in the Research Enquiries Room an index to names in AO 12 which precedes the standard list. In this index the person's name is followed by an abbreviation of the name of the state where the individual claimed to have suffered loss. A volume number and a further number follow these details. The volume number is the same as the piece number that can be found in the left hand column of the list. For example: Ackerly, Isaac, N.Y., V23, 21; in this entry V23 translates into piece 23, and AO 12/23 is the reference to use when ordering the piece on the computer. The second number, 21, is an internal reference which should not be used when requesting the piece. It is the page number in the volume on which the information can be found. The page number in the document is the handwritten number; the printed numbers on the top right hand corner are the folio numbers and do not correlate to the index.

Rolls of declared accounts from the Auditors of the Imprest and the Commissioners of Audit relating to Loyalist claims can be found in AO 1. Papers concerning the claims and some compensation and pension lists of American loyalists and records of the Commissioners constituted to deal with the claims of loyalists and of British merchants under article 6 of the 1794 Treaty of Amity, Commerce and Navigation between Great Britain and the United States, and the convention between the two countries signed in 1802 can be found in Treasury records. T 50: Pay Lists and other Documents concerning Refugees, 1780–1856 and T 79: American Loyalist Claims Commission: Records, 1777–1841 contain the reports of commissioners investigating individual claims, and some compensation and pension lists.

Similar claims for compensation when East Florida was ceded to Spain in 1783 can be found in T 77 for the period 1763–1789. These include reports of the East Florida Claims Commission and lists of title deeds and papers relating to the management of estates. These consist primarily of the claims, with supporting documents, of the settlers of the province of East Florida, which, in 1783, after 20 years of British administration, was ceded to the Crown of Spain under article 5 of the Treaty of Paris. The claimants' papers, usually in the form of a memorial supported by documentation of land grants, indentures, schedules and valuations of property, and often with plans and other maps and plans, make up files 1–18. File 19 consists of reports on the claims of the many settlers who had taken refuge in the Bahamas. Papers relating to the administration of East Florida, in particular with regard to events consequent upon the cession, form file 20. Files 21–30 are largely fragmentary and relate principally to administrative matters, although they do include as well some documentation, including land grants and plans, that has become separated from the main series of claimants' papers (files 1–18): these are not indexed.

## 2.2.3 Land Grant records

In early colonial America the ownership of the land was considered to be vested in the King through the right of discovery and settlement by his subjects. The Monarch in turn granted land to companies and to proprietors to organize settlements and also to some individual subjects as a reward for service. This is further described in O T Barck Jr. and H T Lefler, *Colonial America* (1968).

The system whereby recipients of royal land grants in turn gave or sold land to others varied. In some colonies, notably New England, the legislatures set up by the colonists assumed jurisdiction over the allocation of company lands. They made some direct grants to individuals for 'adventuring' money in the companies but the greater part went to groups or communities to establish townships and apportion the surrounding lands.

In the southern colonies the 'headright' system of land distribution was the most common method followed during the seventeenth century. An individual who provided transportation to the colony of any emigrant was entitled to at least 50 acres of land. During the same period, however, larger tracts were given by the King, proprietor, or company to favourites, to those who performed outstanding service for a company, or, as in Maryland, to those who transported five or more persons to the colony. The 'headright' system led to many frauds and abuses and by the early years of the eighteenth century most of the land was distributed by purchase or by taking out a patent signed by the Governor of a colony for new unpatented land.

No systematic list or comprehensive index exists of the many varied land grants made in colonial America. C M Andrews in his *Guide to the Materials for American History to 1783 in the Public Record Office of Great Britain*, 2 vols (Carnegie Institution, Washington, 1912 and 1914) gives references to the subject generally and to many individual grants. References to other grants can be obtained from the *Journals of the Board of Trade and Plantations*, the *Calendar of State Papers, Colonial, America and West Indies*, and the *Acts of the Privy Council, Colonial Series*, all of which are available for consultation at Kew. Details of the grants referred to in the Journals can be found in the Colonial Office document class CO 5: America and West Indies, Original Correspondence. The records of a great many of the land grants made remained in the colonies and may be available in State archives.

Sources for nineteenth-century land grants can be found in CO 6: North American: Original Correspondence, 1816–1868 and CO 384: Original Correspondence, Emigration, 1817–1896. Settlers in the nineteenth century, mainly British troops already stationed there, applied for land grants and CO 384/51 provides a list of North American settlers, giving personal details of age, career, marital status, children, purpose of application and signature of applicant. This record covers the period 1837–1838.

To establish where regiments were stationed at particular times *see* J M Kitzmuller, *In Search of the 'Forlorn Hope': a Comprehensive Guide to Locating British Regiments and their Records* (Salt Lake City, 1988). This book is available at the Research Enquiries Room desk. Alternatively, consult the following series of records: WO 379: Office of the Commander-in-Chief and War Office: Adjutant General's Office: Disposition and Movement of Regiment, Returns and Papers (Regimental Records), 1737–1950 and WO 380: Office of the Commander-in-Chief and War Office: Adjutant General's Office: Designation, Establishments and Stations of Regiments, Returns and Papers (Regimental Records Series I–IV), 1803–1953. Both series record the location and movement of troops in regiments of the regular and Territorial Army in the United

Kingdom, Ireland and overseas. They are thought to have been maintained by the Adjutant General's Office but latterly were kept in the Ministry of Defence library, where they were probably used to answer historical queries about British regiments. Alternative sources are WO 17: Office of the Commander-in-Chief: Monthly Returns to the Adjutant General, 1759–1865 and WO 73: Office of the Commander-in-Chief and War Office: Distribution of the Army Monthly Returns, 1859–1950. Both series are summarized returns issued by the Quartermaster General, the Adjutant General and the Army Council. They show the distribution of the Army month by month: (a) by divisions and stations and (b) by regiments in numerical order. They give the station of each battalion or company, the numbers of officers and rank and file present or absent and other statistical information.

Land grants relating to the West Indies are described in G Grannum, *Tracing Your West Indian Ancestors* (PRO, 1995). Examples of land grants survive for Bahamas (CO 23/3, 125), Belize (WO 55/1815), the Ceded Islands (CO 76/9, CO 101/1, 11, CO 106/9–12), Dominica (T 1/453), Grenada (CO 101/1), Guyana (CO 111/28, CO 116/73, 75–76), Jamaica (CO 137/28, 162), St Christopher (CO 152/13, T 1/275), St Vincent (T 1/453), Surinam (WO 1/149), and Trinidad (CO 295/35).

### 2.2.4 War brides and war babies

One of the largest groups of emigrants to the US and Canada in the twentieth century is Second World War brides. It is estimated that over a million US GIs (Government Issues) and Canadian servicemen were stationed in Britain during the Second World War and that in excess of 80,000 British women became their war brides. Although there is no central complete listing of war brides, entries for them should be found in Board of Trade Outward Passenger Lists in BT 27 (*see* 1.3). Also, the printed indexes to the general correspondence of the Foreign Office (FO) contain information relating to the passage of war brides to Canada and the US – because of tight immigration laws a special act of Congress needed to be passed in the US in 1947 to facilitate their migration. Useful web sites for Canadian war brides include http://canadianwarbrides.com and for GI brides www.pastonroot.co.uk/golds/448-gib.html.

It is not clear how many babies were the products of wartime affairs that ended with the American and Canadian fathers shipping out of Britain; estimates range from 20,000 to 50,000. TRACE (Transatlantic Children's Enterprise) is a non-profit making self-help support group whose aim is to help people trace their GI/Canadian fathers/families. Information about TRACE can be found at http://freespace.virgin.net/j.munro/trace.htm.

## 2.3 Emigration to Australia and New Zealand – special sources

European settlement of Australia began with the penal colony at Botany Bay on the east coast of Australia in 1788. *See* Chapter 4 for records relating to prisoners transported overseas.

Australia also attracted free settlers, though in the PRO there are few records relating to voluntary emigrants to Australia and New Zealand until the Passenger Lists (BT 27) begin in 1890 (*see* 1.3 and 1.4).

Aside from the general Colonial Office sources referred to in 2.1, CO 201: New South Wales Original Correspondence, 1783–1900, includes lists of settlers, 1801–1821. The correspondence of 1823 to 1833 has also been indexed in a supplementary finding aid to this series, available in the Research Enquiries Room. CO 386: Land and Emigration Commission, etc., 1833–1894, contains original correspondence and entry books of the Agent General for Emigration, the South Australian Commissioners and the Land and Emigration Commission.

Names of Australian settlers can also be traced in CO 202: New South Wales Entry Books, 1786–1873, CO 360: New South Wales Register of Correspondence, 1849–1900 and CO 368: New South Wales Register of Out-Letters, 1873–1900. Similarly, names of New Zealand settlers can be traced in CO 209: New Zealand Original Correspondence, 1830–1922.

The censuses of New South Wales and Tasmania conducted at intervals between 1788 and 1859 are valuable sources (*see* 5.2.6). Although primarily conducted to record convict details, the censuses do include the names of individuals who 'came free' or who were 'born in the colony'.

Microfilms of many PRO documents referred to in this section are available in Australia at the National Library in Canberra, and at the Mitchell Library in Sydney.

The National Archives of Australia (NAA), web site www.naa.gov.au, holds records relating to Australia's schemes to sponsor British migrants prior to the Second World War and after. Such schemes included the 'Group Settlement' and 'Land Settlement' schemes, and the famous '£10 Pom' scheme. This scheme ran from 1950 to 1973 and selected case studies can be found at the National Library in Canberra.

The Genealogical Society of Victoria has catalogues and microfiche collections relating to free, assisted and non-assisted immigration to Australia, with sources relating to settlement in Victoria (from 1835), New South Wales (from 1835), South Australia (from 1836), Tasmania (from 1804) and Northern Territory (from 1824). They also have various fiche collections relating to settlement in New Zealand from 1840 after British sovereignty was declared.

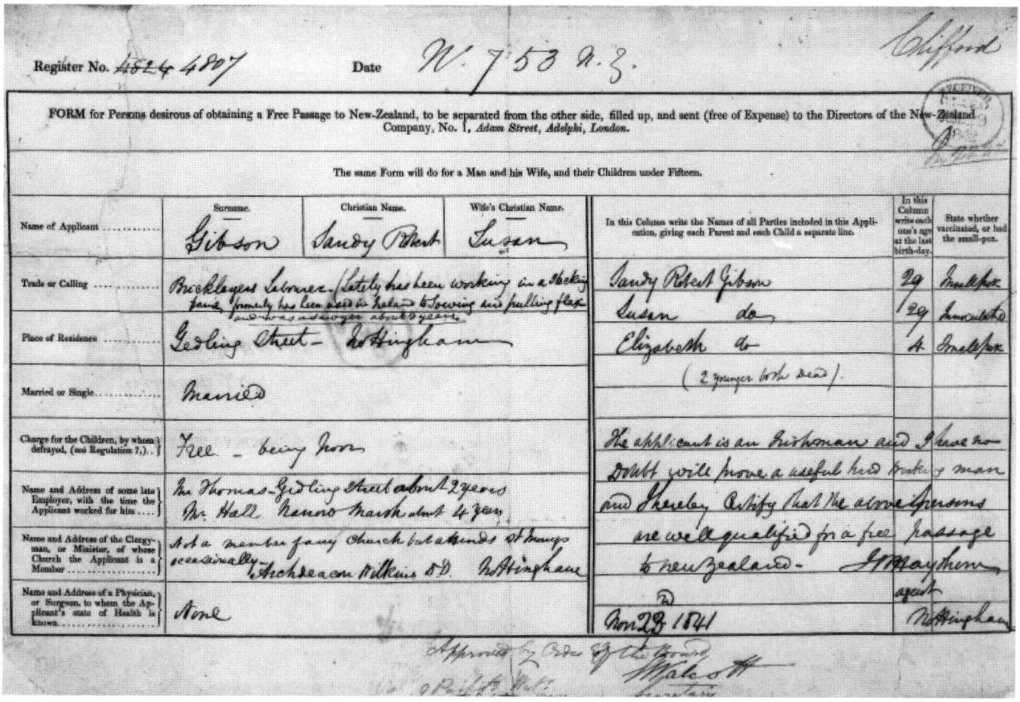

Register No. 4524 4807 Date N. 7 53 n. 3.

FORM for Persons desirous of obtaining a Free Passage to New-Zealand, to be separated from the other side, filled up, and sent (free of Expense) to the Directors of the New-Zealand Company, No. 1, *Adam Street, Adelphi, London.*

The same Form will do for a Man and his Wife, and their Children under Fifteen.

| | Surname. | Christian Name. | Wife's Christian Name. | In this Column write the Names of all Parties included in this Application, giving each Parent and each Child a separate line. | In this Column write each one's age at the last birth-day. | State whether vaccinated, or had the small-pox. |
|---|---|---|---|---|---|---|
| Name of Applicant | Gibson | Sandy Robert | Susan | Sandy Robert Gibson | 29 | Small pox |
| Trade or Calling | Bricklayers Labourer | | | Susan do | 29 | |
| Place of Residence | Gedling Street – Nottingham | | | Elizabeth do | 4 | Small pox |
| Married or Single | Married | | | ( 2 younger both dead ) | | |
| Charge for the Children, by whom defrayed, (see Regulation 7.) | Free – being born | | | | | |
| Name and Address of some late Employer, with the time the Applicant worked for him | Mr Thomas – Gedling Street about 2 years; Mr Hall | | | | | |
| Name and Address of the Clergyman, or Minister, of whose Church the Applicant is a Member | Archdeacon Wilkins DD. Nottingham | | | | | |
| Name and Address of a Physician, or Surgeon, to whom the Applicant's state of Health is known | None | | | Nov 23 1841 | | |

Figure 17 Application for free passage to New Zealand by Sandy Robert Gibson and his family, March 1841 (CO 208/274 (pt 2), fol. 324)

## 2.3.1 New Zealand Company records

New Zealand was not used as a penal colony. Details of emigrants may be found in CO 208: New Zealand Company Original Correspondence, 1839–1858. The New Zealand Company was formed in 1839 and incorporated in 1841 with power to buy, sell, settle and cultivate land in New Zealand. It surrendered its charter in 1850 and was dissolved in 1858. This series of records contains registers of cabin passengers emigrating, 1839–1850, in CO 208/269–272, applications for free passage, 1839–1850, in CO 208/273–274 (indexed in CO 208/275), applications for land, lists of landowners, in CO 208/254–255, lists of agents and surveyors, lists of German emigrants and lists of maintained emigrants.

## 2.3.2 Land purchases and free passages

In CO 386: Land and Emigration Commission Papers, 1833–1894, there are documents, such as CO 386/21, giving the regulations governing the colonization of Australia through the Wakefield Scheme of 1829, whereby land was sold for a substantial price in the colony, and the funds thus generated used to ship emigrant

**86**

(Copy.)

# SOUTH AUSTRALIA.
## Peculiar Land Order. (Part 1.)

No. *91*

IN pursuance of the provisions of the Act 4 & 5
WILLIAM IV. c. 95, intituled "An Act to empower His Majesty
"to erect South Australia into a British Province or Provinces,
"and to provide for the Colonization and Government thereof,"—

*John Ward Esqre*

of *Bedford Street Covent Garden*
hath paid for One Section of Rural Land, consisting of Eighty
Acres; and also for Ten other Acres of Town Land, forming a
portion of the 9,000 Acres purchased by certain Directors of an
Association for the purchase of one or more special survey or
surveys of Land in South Australia, and for which an Order for a
special survey or surveys, dated the 21st December, 1838, was
issued by the Colonization Commissioners for South Australia,
addressed to the Resident Commissioner of Public Lands; and
which Ninety Acres of Land is to be taken by the said

*John Ward*

with such privileges, and subject to such stipulations, as are
mentioned in the said Order, dated the 21st December, 1838.  So
soon as the said Land shall have been selected, you are to put
him, his Agent, or Assigns, into possession thereof, and to procure
a grant thereof, to be made to him, his Heirs, and Assigns, subject
to the laws and regulations of the Colony.  *This Land Order is
issued in Duplicate, and upon the presentation of either Copy,
the other will become void.*

Dated London, this *3rd* day of *May* 1839.

}  Colonization Commissioners
   for South Australia.

Secretary.

Entered, *JB.*

To the Resident Commissioner of Public Lands
of the Colony of South Australia.

RECEIVED this *29* day of *May* 1839,
the Land Order of which the above is a Copy. *for John
Ward*                    (Signed)

*Wm. G. Gove*

**Figure 18** South Australia Peculiar Land Orders: No 91, John Ward of Bedford Street, Covent Garden (CO 386/146)

labourers from Britain to work the land. Those purchasing the land were assured of an adequate supply of labour of the right type, since labourers were vetted before being given the passage. The labourer was promised a new and more prosperous life in a colony where labour was in demand, while prospects were poor at home. The scheme proposed to set up a colony along approved lines and at the same time relieve unemployment and pauperism at home.

The South Australian Colonization Commission, a predecessor of the Land and Emigration Commission, was responsible for laying down the regulations for land sales and overseeing the selection of emigrants eligible for a free passage.

The documents CO 386/142–143, 145–146 and 148–152 contain information relating to the Wakefield Scheme, the South Australian Colonization Commission, the sale of land in Australia to individuals and labourers' applications for free passages.

*See* 2.3.1 for New Zealand land purchases and free passages.

### 2.3.3 *Army pensioners*

Between 1846 and 1851, Army pensioners were encouraged to settle in New South Wales and New Zealand, although many of them failed as settlers. References to the settlement of ex-soldiers in Australia and New Zealand will be found in the PRO's *Alphabetical Guide to Certain War Office and Other Military Records (List and Index volume 8)*, under *Australia* and *New Zealand*.

WO 43: War Office: Secretary-at-War, Correspondence, Very Old Series (VOS), and Old Series (OS), 1809–1857, contain papers relating to particular emigrant officers and soldiers in relation to half-pay, pensions, annuities and allowances. Similarly, references to former soldiers who settled in any colony can be found in WO 22: Royal Hospital Chelsea: Pensions Returns, 1842–1883. *See* 2.1.3 for more information regarding this series.

Reference to ex-soldier emigrants, 1830–1848, to Australia can be found in WO 43/542. Similarly, WO 43/543 relates to New Zealand returns. Pension return records for District Offices survive for New South Wales, 1849–1880 in WO 22/272–275; for South Australia, Queensland, Tasmania and Victoria, 1876–1880 in WO 22/227, 297, 298 and 300; and for New Zealand, 1845–1854 and 1875–1880 in WO 22/276–293.

## 2.4  Emigration to South Africa – special sources

After some dispute as to ownership of the Cape of Good Hope between colonial powers, the territory was recaptured by the British from the Dutch in 1806 and formally became a British colony in 1814. In 1843 Natal was declared a British colony and by 1902 Britain had gained control of the former Boer republics of the Orange Free State and Transvaal. In 1910 Cape Colony, Orange River Colony, Natal and Transvaal united to form the new Union of South Africa. All provinces attracted British settlers.

CO 48: Cape of Good Hope Colony (Cape Colony), Original Correspondence, 1807–1910, contains letters from settlers and papers about grants of land at the Cape of Good Hope, 1814–1825. For the same colony, there are CO 49: Cape of Good Hope Colony (Cape Colony), Entry Books, 1795–1872, CO 336: Cape of Good Hope (Cape Colony) Register of Correspondence, 1850–1910 and CO 462: Cape of Good Hope (Cape Colony) Register of Out-letters, 1872–1910. All series contain reference to individual settlers.

There are two excellent published works relating to British settlers in South Africa: P Philip, *British Residents at the Cape, 1795–1819* (Cape Town, 1981), and E Bull, *Aided Immigration from Britain to South Africa, 1857–1867* (Pretoria, 1991). Both have compiled lists of settlers using original sources and provide information relating to particular nineteenth-century emigration schemes such as the Byrne Settlers who came from all over the UK to Natal. A useful website for South African genealogy is www.sun.ac.za/gisa/bronne.htm.

For settlers after 1910, when South Africa became the Union of South Africa, individual files on immigrants are available via the Department of Home Affairs in South Africa, Private Bag X114, Pretoria, 0001, South Africa.

### 2.4.1  War Office records

WO 148: Civilian Claims to Military Compensation Boards, South African War, 1900–1905, contain a representative selection of registers, indexes, and files relating to claims made by civilians to the Central and District Military Compensation Boards in respect of losses suffered by reason of the South African War, or for property requisitioned by the military forces.

Registers of payments to Army and Navy pensioners (including some widows and orphans) at the Cape of Good Hope and elsewhere in South Africa, 1849–1858 and 1876–1880, are in WO 22/243–244. The muster rolls of the Cape Levies, 1851–1853, may prove useful (WO 13/3718–3725).

## 2.5 Emigration to India – special sources

The British Library, Oriental and India Office Collections, 96 Euston Road, London NW1 2DB (Tel: 020 7412 7873, web site: www.bl.uk) holds records relating to the British administration of India prior to independence in 1947.

The records comprise the archives of the East India Company (1600–1858), of the Board of Control or Board of Commissioners for the Affairs of India (1784–1858), of the India Office (1858–1947), of the Burma Office (1937–1948) and of a number of related British agencies overseas. The India Office records are administered by The British Library as part of the public records of the United Kingdom, and are open for public consultation under the provisions of the Public Record Acts and in accordance with regulations established by the Lord Chancellor.

The Oriental and India Office Collections contain extensive records of India for both the period 1600 to 1858, when the East India Company (*see* 2.5.1.1) controlled the region, and from 1858 to 1947, when India was ruled by the British government through the India Office. Among the numerous sources there is a card index with details of nearly 300,000 civil and military personnel, their families and others. The collections also contain registers of births, marriages and burials, arranged by presidency (Bengal, Bombay, Madras), registered wills of the three presidencies, railway employees, and service records for military personnel in the East India Company and the Indian Army. The PRO Library and Resource Centre holds a run of the annual *East India Register*, continued by the *India List* (under various titles) from 1791–1947, as well as the separate *Indian Army Lists*.

The Society of Genealogists, 14 Charterhouse Buildings, Goswell Road, London EC1M 7BA, has an excellent collection of material relating to emigration to India, including birth, marriage and death announcements (and obituaries) extracted from Indian newspapers.

Also, consult http://members.ozemail.com.au/~clday, a web site for people tracing their British, European and Anglo-Indian family history in India, Burma, Pakistan and Bangladesh.

### 2.5.1 *Company and Society records*

#### 2.5.1.1 East India Company

The East India Company was established in 1600 as a joint-stock association of English merchants who received, by a series of charters, exclusive rights to trade to the East Indies. The East Indies were defined as the lands lying between the Cape of

Good Hope and the Straits of Magellan, and the Company soon established a network of warehouses or 'factories' throughout south and east Asia. Over a period of 250 years the Company underwent several substantial changes in its basic character and functions. A period of rivalry between the Old and New Companies after 1698 resulted in the formation in 1709 of the United Company of Merchants Trading to the East Indies. This 'new' East India Company was transformed during the second half of the eighteenth century from a mainly commercial body with scattered Asian trading interests into a major territorial power in India with its headquarters in Calcutta. The political implications of this development eventually caused the British government in 1784 to institute standing Commissioners (the Board of Control) in London to exercise supervision over the Company's Indian policies. This change in the Company's status, along with other factors, led to the Acts of Parliament of 1813 and 1833 which opened British trade with the East Indies to all shipping and resulted in the Company's complete withdrawal from its commercial functions. The Company continued to exercise responsibility, under the supervision of the Board, for the government of India until the re-organization of 1858.

Throughout most of these changes the basic structure of Company organization in East India House in the City of London remained largely unaltered, comprising a large body of proprietors or shareholders and an elected Court of Directors, headed by a chairman and deputy chairman who, aided by permanent officials, were responsible for the daily conduct of Company business. The Board of Control maintained its separate office close to the Government buildings in Westminster.

With the India Act of 1858 the Company and the Board of Control were replaced by a single new department of state, the India Office, which functioned, under the Secretary of State for India, as an executive office of United Kingdom government alongside the Foreign Office, Colonial Office, Home Office and War Office. The Secretary of State was assisted by a statutory body of advisers, the Council of India, and headed a staff of civil servants organized into a system of departments largely taken over from the East India Company and Board of Control establishments, and housed in a new India Office building in Whitehall. The Secretary of State for India inherited all the executive functions previously carried out by the Company, and all the powers of 'superintendence, direction and control' over the British Government in India previously exercised by the Board of Control. Improved communications with India – the overland and submarine telegraph cables (1868–70), and the opening of the Suez Canal (1869) – rendered this control, exercised through the Viceroy and provincial Governors, more effective in the last quarter of the nineteenth century. It was only with the constitutional reforms initiated during the First World War, and carried forward by the India Acts of 1919 and 1935, that there came about a significant relaxation of India Office supervision over the Government of India, and with it, in India, a gradual devolution of authority to legislative bodies and local governments. The same administrative reforms also led in 1937 to the separation of Burma from

India and the creation in London of the Burma Office, separate from the India Office though sharing the same Secretary of State and located in the same building. With the grant of independence to India and Pakistan in 1947, and to Burma in 1948, both the India Office and the Burma Office were dissolved.

The vast majority of East India Company records are held at the British Library, Oriental and India Office Collections, 96 Euston Road, London NW1 2DB (Tel: 020 7412 7873, web site: www.bl.uk). Access to some of their catalogues is available via their web site.

The *European Manuscripts* collection of the India Office Library houses the private papers of several hundred people who served in India, including Viceroys and Governors, civil servants, army officers and other ranks, businessmen, missionaries, scholars, travellers and their families. This growing collection (now over 16,000 volumes) of letters, diaries, papers of all kinds and tape-recordings supplements the official records and illustrates the wide diversity of work and social life in India and neighbouring countries since 1650.

The PRO holds the series of records FO 41: General Correspondence before 1906, East India Company, 1776–1797, which consist of correspondence with the Court of Directors of the East India Company. Also available at the PRO is the series CO 77: East Indies Original Correspondence, Entry Books, 1570–1856. This series contains original correspondence and entries relating to the East Indies and includes documents relating to Persia and China, and to the embassy to China of 1793 to 1794.

The *Calendar of State Papers East Indies, 1513–1668* (5 vols) calendars material available at both the British Library and the PRO. Copies of the calendars are available in the Research Enquiries Room.

### 2.5.1.2 Indian Railway Companies

Available at The British Library Oriental and India Office Collections are records of appointments in the United Kingdom to employment in Indian Railway Companies 1848–1925: L/AG/46/4, L/AG/46/10–12 and L/AG/46/18 series. For these records there is separate card index in the reading room.

## 2.5.2 Indian Army records

Also available at the Oriental and India Office Collections are personal records relating to the Queen's India Cadetships 1858–1930: L/MIL/9/292–302, Sandhurst cadets commissioned into the Indian Army Unattached List 1859–1940: L/MIL/9/303–319, and Quetta cadets 1915–1918: L/MIL/9/320–332.

For records of service for officers, surgeons, departmental warrant officers, NCOs and privates, see I A Baxter *Brief Guide to Bibliographical Sources in the India Office Library*. For officers of the Bengal Army 1758–1834, see V C P Hodson, *List of the Officers of the Bengal Army*, 4 vols (London, 1927–1947). For surgeons, see D G Crawford, *Roll of the Indian Medical Service 1615–1930* (London, 1930). Also available at the Oriental and India Office Collections are assistant Surgeons and Surgeons' papers 1804–1914: L/MIL/9/358–408.

The PRO Library and Resource Centre holds a run of the annual *Indian Army Lists*.

### 2.5.3 Indian Civil Service records

Again, these records are available at the Oriental and India Office Collections and include an incomplete series of writers' petitions 1749–1856, and appointment papers for East India Company civil servants with baptismal certificates and educational testimonials. Brief service records for high-ranking civil servants appear in the *India Office List* 1886–1947 in the Reading Room. (The PRO Library and Resource Centre holds a run of the annual *East India Register*, continued by the *India List* (under various titles) from 1791–1947.)

Histories of Service (V/12 series) for higher-ranking officers from 1879 give promotions and postings, sometimes dates of birth. Civil Lists (V/13 series) for lower-rank officials from 1840 do not give a continuous career record, and searchers consequently need to consult a sequence of annual volumes to establish an individual's career.

Records of personnel employed in government railways, police, public works, post office, etc. 1818–1900, 1922–1928 can be found in L/F/10 series. Name, occupation, salary and period of residence in India are usually provided in these records. Deaths in the Uncovenanted Civil Service 1870–1949 are found in L/AG/34/14A. These records give name of deceased, date and place of death, rank, age, native town and country, next of kin, custody of property if any. There is a separate card index in the Reading Room.

## 2.6 Emigration to South America – special sources

### 2.6.1 Patagonia

In 1865 a Welsh-speaking colony, called in Welsh 'Y Wladfa' ('The Colony'), was established in the valley of the Chubut River in Patagonia in Argentina. The original emigrants sailed from Liverpool on the *Mimosa*. In the 1880s a further colony was established in the foothills of the Andes and this was called 'Cwm Hyfryd' ('Pleasant Valley'). Although measures were later taken to remove some of the colonists to Canada and South Africa, most of the settlers and their descendants remained in Argentina.

A memorandum on Patagonia is kept at the Research Enquiries Room enquiry desk listing PRO documents concerned with the colony. A search on PROCAT using the terms 'Patagonia', 'Chubut' and 'Chupat' reveals some interesting sources from various departmental codes including ADM (Admiralty), FO (Foreign Office), HO (Home Office) and SP (State Papers Department).

## 2.7 Emigration to the Middle East – special sources

### 2.7.1 The Levant Company records

The Levant Company was established in 1581 when its members were granted a monopoly of English trade with the Turkish Empire. Its representative at the Turkish court at Constantinople was also given diplomatic authority as English ambassador. Subsequently, consulates, manned by representatives of the Company, were appointed at strategic trading posts throughout the western Turkish Empire, including Aleppo, Algiers, Cairo, Chios, Patras, Salonika, Smyrna, Tunis and Zante.

By the second half of the eighteenth century, the Levant Company was in financial difficulties and could no longer afford to maintain the ambassador and consuls without government subsidy. In 1804, the Foreign Office took over full responsibility for the British embassy at Constantinople and the Company appointed its own consul general to look after its commercial interests.

The consuls had enforced the ordinances of the company throughout the Levant, levied consulage on imports and exports, maintained law and order, adjudicated disputes, administered the estates of Englishmen who died abroad and exercised control over the factors who were the local representatives of merchants based in London. Large factories, such as in Aleppo, also appointed a salaried treasurer and a chancellor, who recorded all the official business of the factory and registered all acts, contracts and wills made by the factors.

SP 105: Secretaries of State: State Papers Foreign, Archives of British Legations, 1568–1871 consists of letter books and correspondence of British embassies and legations abroad mainly to the year 1796. The series includes records of the Levant Company's London-based governing body, the General Court, and its officers, including minute books of the General Court (1611 to 1706); letter books of instructions to ambassadors, consuls and other agents (1606 to 1825) and treasurer's accounts. Of the Company's diplomatic and consular missions only Constantinople, Aleppo, Smyrna and Cairo are represented.

Amongst the miscellaneous records of British envoys, agents and ambassadors are the letter books of Sir Balthasar Gerbier, minister at Brussels (1631 to 1642); correspondence of the commissioners appointed to oversee the demolition of the fortifications of Dunkirk under the terms of the Treaty of Utrecht; letter books of the Secretary of State concerning peace negotiations at Utrecht (1711 to 1714); letter books of missions involved in peace negotiations with France (1698 to 1772) and missions to the Imperial Diet and states within the Holy Roman Empire.

Also included are the collections of the correspondence and papers of individual diplomats, notably Sir George Stepney (1663 to 1707) concerning his missions to German states and the Holy Roman Empire, and Sir Joseph Williamson (1633 to 1701) and Sir Leoline Jenkins (1623 to 1685) concerning their negotiations at the congresses of Cologne (1673) and Nimeguen (1676). Correspondence of the resident minister at the court of Tuscany includes dispatches from the government agent Philip von Stosch concerning the movements of the Old Pretender and the Jacobite court.

Levant Company out-letter books to 1670 are described in the Calendar of State Papers (Domestic Series) of the reign of Charles II; these are available in the Map and Large Document Room for consultation.

### 2.7.2 The British Mandate in the Middle East

#### 2.7.2.1 Palestine

Between 1920 and 1948, Palestine was administered by the United Kingdom under a League of Nations (later United Nations) mandate. For most of this time, the mandate territories were run by a Government of Palestine, which employed local residents and, especially in the police service, the railways and port authority, UK and Commonwealth citizens. Many of these built up pension entitlements, which after the end of the mandate became the responsibility of the Colonial Office. Administration and payment of the pensions passed to the Crown Agents and then to the Department for Technical Co-operation. The records used to administer the pensions are now held by the Department for International Development, Abercrombie House, Eaglesham Road, East Kilbride, Glasgow G75 8EA, which still administers the pensions. After the end of the mandate, a trust fund set up to provide for the dependants of those killed or wounded by terrorist action in Palestine was administered by a committee for which the Colonial Office provided the secretary.

The card index and register of pensioners are vital finding aids to the service files and service cards. The service cards principally document the service of locally engaged Government of Palestine staff, while the service files are principally those of UK and old Commonwealth staff, and include the service cards plus other service details (medical, leave entitlement, pay, etc.). All the cards include attached photographs. The largest block of records is the service files: there are about 8,000 of these.

These records are likely to be of huge interest to genealogists and, at the time of writing this Guide, the PRO Records Management Department (RMD) had agreed the following course of action:

> The war medal list is of a type with other similar lists already held by the PRO, and will be acquired here. The list documents a very specific interaction of the state with individuals, and it would mean that this list could be studied along with other similar lists already held by the PRO.

> The minutes of the Committee on Palestine Public Service (Supplementary Grants) Trust, 1949–1960, record the work of a Colonial Office funded and run committee. These are the original records of the committee, and the PRO does not already hold copies. They will be acquired to show the UK's continuing relations with the successor states on the difficult issue of the status and position of servants of the former government after the end of the mandate.

> The service records, cards and finding aids would be a popular acquisition, but it would be hard to justify their acquisition under current PRO policy. The PRO will seek an appropriate place of deposit for the records.

> These proposals would not mean splitting a collection as the records form distinct series of collections. The medal list and Committee records are not required to access the service records.

> The pension records and service files will be offered first to the Middle East Centre at St Anthony's College in Oxford, which has approached the Palestine Police Association and indicated that it would be a willing recipient. In the event of St Anthony's proving either unwilling or unsuitable to receive the records, other possible recipients will be sought. In the event of no suitable recipient being found, the RMD Panel will consider the records afresh to determine if the PRO should acquire them.

PRO file CO 733/489/1 records the destruction, either in Palestine in April 1948, or in the UK subsequently, of all classified Government of Palestine papers not required for further administrative purposes. Films of some records of the Accountant General's Department and the Custodian of Enemy Property for Palestine were made in 1948, and passed to the Crown Agents (CO 733/494/2). The originals of these copies, and other originals, can be assumed never to have left Palestine, being either destroyed *in situ*, or passing into the hands of the successor states, though there is no evidence of this on file.

### 2.7.2.2 Iraq

Included among the other territories of the former German and Ottoman Empires, given under mandate by the League of Nations to the Allied Powers to administer, was Iraq. For records relating to this mandate see CO 696: Iraq: Sessional papers, 1917–1931; CO 730: Iraq: Original Correspondence, 1921–1932; and CO 781: Iraq: Register of Correspondence, 1921–1932. The remaining mandates were in Africa in the Cameroons and Tanganyika.

# 3 Child Emigration Schemes

British child emigration schemes operated from 1618 to 1967. During this period it was estimated that some 150,000 children were sent to the British Colonies and Dominions, most notably America, Australia, and Canada, but also Rhodesia, New Zealand, South Africa and the Caribbean. Many of the children were in the care of the voluntary organizations who arranged for their emigration. Child emigration peaked from the 1870s until 1914, and some 80,000 children were sent to Canada alone during this period.

The aim of child emigration was often to increase the population within the Colonies, and to improve labour and productivity there. Although most schemes were presented as being for the benefit and the welfare of the child, few schemes actually took the feelings of the children into account.

## 3.1  Records in the UK

For its part, the UK Government has considered that such policies and schemes were misguided and, as a direct result of the House of Commons 1997–8 Third Report from the Health Select Committee into the Welfare of Former Child Migrants, the British Government announced in 1999 several measures to assist former British child emigrants to trace their personal records and travel to the UK to reunite with close family, from whom they were separated and with whom they lost contact when they emigrated to Australia.

The Government has therefore set up two new kinds of help: the Child Migrant Central Information Index, and the Support Fund.

### 3.1.1  The Child Migrant Central Information Index

The Child Migrant Central Information Index contains basic information about individual child emigrants taken from the available UK records of known sending agencies. The Index acts as a signpost to the sending agencies holding personal records. The Index, initially funded for three years from April 1999, is available to former child emigrants themselves, parents and siblings of child emigrants and any nominated representatives. As access is restricted, the Index will not be made available over the Internet. Initially, the Index relates to those child emigrants who were sent to Australia, Canada and New Zealand on government-assisted schemes between 1920 and the late 1960s. It will not be a complete listing of all former child emigrants and may not lead some people to locate their original records for the following reasons: the records were destroyed during the Second World War; the agency may no longer exist and may not have transferred their records to another repository for preservation; some records may have been lost; some agencies may not have been very clear in identifying some emigrants as children; problems may arise from poor transcripts or handwriting.

Further enquiries about the index should be made to the National Council of Voluntary Child Care Organisations, Unit 4, Pride Court, 80–82 White Lion Street, London N1 9PF. Tel/Fax: 020 7713 5937; e-mail: migrant@voluntarychild.org; web site www.voluntarychild.org.

### 3.1.2 The Support Fund

The Support Fund was set up to help those without means who have found their family and who wish to travel to the UK for a first-time reunion with their families. At the time of publication, this fund is available for three years from April 1999. The UK contact address for the Fund is the International Social Services (ISS) UK, Cranmer House, 39 Brixton Road, London SW9 6DD. Tel: 020 7735 8941/4, Fax: 020 7582 0696.

Additional records about child emigrants may be held in the recipient countries, such as Australia (*see* 3.2.1), Canada (*see* 3.2.2), and New Zealand.

### 3.1.3 Home Office records

Before 1972, responsibility for the application of various Acts relating to children lay with the Home Office. MH 102 consists of policy files in the Home Office six-figure registered file series. These cover all aspects of child detention in remand homes and industrial and approved schools, including subjects such as absconding, education, general health and welfare, boarding out, fostering and adoption, holiday camps, emigration, employment and after-care. Related policy files in the CHN (Children) series, which originated in the Home Office in 1949, can be found in BN 29 and BN 62, with representative case files in BN 28, though the vast majority of these files are closed for 75 years. Earlier files can be found in general series of Home Office registered papers in HO 45 and HO 144, under the subject cuts, *Children* and *Emigration*. Although comprising mainly policy and correspondence files relating to the emigration of children under the Children Act, 1908, ch. 67, the records also include schemes for the emigration of children to Canada and Australia.

203442

ROWE,     EVA MAY SELINA,   now aged 13.
  "       HILDA KATE,       now aged 9.

Committed on 26th November 1907 under 4 Edward Vll Chapter
15.
Father living.

Committed at Southampton, at Petty Sessional Court, by
Magistrates for Borough and County.

---

The mother died in November 1905.   The father, a painter,
was said to be of lazy and drunken habits.   In March 1906, he was
sentenced to three months hard labour for having neglected his
children.   The neglect, however, was subsequently resumed, and in
November 1907 the father was sentenced to six months hard labour for
having neglected his children, who had undergone the severest priva-
tions, and were found to be living under the most wretched conditions
and in a state bordering on starvation.

---

Memoranda.

A notice - copy attached - of the proposed emigration of
these girls was sent to the father on the 20th inst., and the accom-
panying letter has been received from him in reply.   It is hoped,
that, in view of the facts mentioned above, the Secretary of State
will see his way clear to sanction the emigration of the children,
notwithstanding the father's objection.

**Figure 19**  Dr Barnardo's Home, Home Office reports: the case of the proposed
emigration of sisters Eva Mary Selina Rowe (aged 13) and Hilda Kate Rowe (aged 9)
in November 1907 (HO 144/1118/203442)

203442

Copy

HOME OFFICE
2? JAN 1911
RECEIVED

18 to 26, Stepney Causeway,
London, E.
20th January 1911.

To Mr G. Rowe,

I am desired by the Managers of these Institutions
to inform you that your daughters , Eva May and Hilda Kate Rowe,
now in the Girls' Village Home, Barkingside, Ilford,  will
probably be selected to go with the next Party of children to
our Branch Home in Canada, from which place they will, if they
behave well, be received into a Canadian family and find a
happy home.

Should you desire to write to the children, their
address is - c/o The Secretary, Margaret Cox Girls' Home,
Peterboro', Ontario, Canada.  Your letters will only need a penny
stamp if they do not exceed an ounce in weight

The Managers will be pleased to furnish you at
intervals with tidings of their progress and welfare in the
new country.

I am directed to inform you that in Canada they
will be under the same kind and watchful supervision, on the
part of experienced ladies belonging to our Home, as they would
have enjoyed had they remained in England.  The Managers have
every reason to believe that their best interests will be secured
by their emigration.

I am,

Yours faithfully,

( Signed )          George Code

Honorary Secretary

**Figure 19** (cont.)

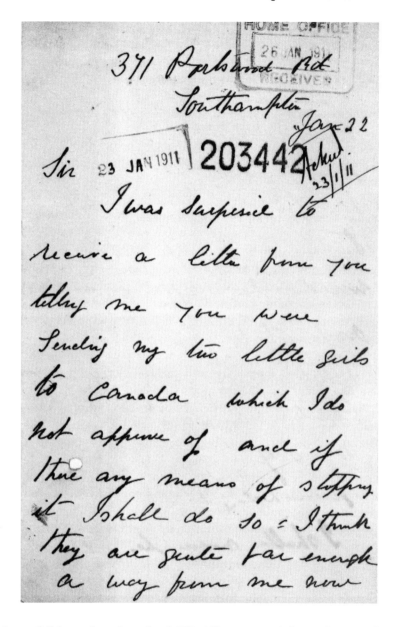

**Figure 19** (cont.)

The records concerning child emigration in MH 102 are mainly policy and correspondence files relating to schemes between 1910 and 1960 set up by the UK, South Africa, Canada, New Zealand and Australia. Records include movements set up by Dr Barnardo's Homes, the Fairbridge Society, the Overseas Migration Board, and the Big Brother emigration scheme, a voluntary organization set up in 1925 for the purpose of fostering the emigration of boys to Australia aged 16 and 17 and 'big brothering' them until the age of at least 21. The Big Brother scheme attracted over 2,000 children before the Second World War and a further 1,400 between 1947 and

1954. The boys, recruited through UK press publicity and applications to orphanages, were selected to work in trades in Tasmania and New South Wales. The boys mainly worked in the agricultural industry and were each allotted a big brother to take the place of family and friends until the age of 21.

Some personnel files are closed for 75 or 100 years, including MH 102/2254 which contains detailed lists of children sailing for Australia under the Fairbridge Society scheme in 1950–54. Most of the records within the series HO 144: Registered Files, Supplementary Series, are subject to extended closure.

### 3.1.4 Emigration of pauper children

The earliest evidence of poor children emigrating overseas is in 1617 when the Virginia Company in America asked for children to be sent to their colony. The City of London responded by sending over 100 poor and orphaned children from Christ's Hospital School and school registers in the custody of the Guildhall Library, Aldermanbury, London EC2P 2EJ include the names of some 1,000 children who were sent to America.

It was estimated that in the mid-eighteenth century, one in three of all paupers was under 16. This put an enormous strain on Poor Law authorities who could not find apprenticeships for all pauper children. The Poor Law Amendment Act 1850, cap cI, allowed Boards of Guardians to send children under 16 overseas for the first time (though it was not until 1870 that the majority of schemes began to take place).

One of the first parties of young paupers to be taken to Canada was led by the Evangelical, Maria Rye. Annie Macpherson, with Maria Rye, had opened a school for destitute children in London and Liverpool in 1870 and most of her emigrants came from these institutions rather than workhouse schools. Such schemes (like those carried out by other voluntary groups such as Dr Barnado's, and the Canadian Catholic Emigration Committee) had to arrange for the reception of the children in Canada, and for their subsequent settlement in suitable families. In 1874, the Local Government Board (LGB) despatched an inspector to Canada to assess the conditions of emigration and welfare arrangements. The inspector, Andrew Doyle, was critical of a number of points, one of which was the high demand of physical work in the farmsteads which was being put upon children as young as seven. As a result of the Doyle report, in March 1875 the LGB withdrew its approval of pauper child emigration, though voluntary organizations continued to send non-pauper children. In 1884, on the condition that certain welfare conditions were met, the LGB relaxed its prohibition on pauper child emigration. The sending of the children and their eventual placement remained the responsibility of the sending agencies.

During the First World War there was a temporary cessation of child emigration and by 1920 mass emigration of lone pauper children to Canada had effectively ended. Over 80,000 children had emigrated to the Dominion of Canada since 1870.

There are few PRO documents available that record child emigrants for this period. LGB Poor Law records in MH 12 tend only to record statistical information on the numbers of children sent overseas, though they sometimes include Poor Law Union posters giving notice of the names and ages of children being sent abroad. Archives of the voluntary agencies may provide more details. Maria Rye's records can be found among the records of the Church of England Children's Bureau, Edward Rudolf House, Margery Street, London WC1X OJL. Annie Macpherson's records and those relating to the work of Dr Barnardo's are in the custody of the Department of Special Collections and Archives (Social Works Archives), Sydney Jones Library, the University of Liverpool, PO Box 123, Liverpool L69 3DA. These records include registers of child emigrants and case files. Such personal archives are subject to access restrictions. The closed period is usually 100 years. In addition to these archives, Barnardo's retains an extensive archive of some 400,000 photographs detailing the work of the charity. The photographs date from 1866. Further information is available at Barnardo's Photographic and Film Archive, Tanners Lane, Barkingside, Ilford, Essex, IG6 1QL.

MH 19: Local Government Board and predecessors: Correspondence with Government Offices, 1834–1909, contains correspondence of the Poor Law Commission and Board and the Local Government Board with other government departments, the Metropolitan Police, the Metropolitan Board of Works and parliamentary officers relating to Poor Law administration and, after 1871, public health and local government services.

The series includes volumes of internal correspondence and papers of the Poor Law Board and the Local Government Board (LGB), including draft orders and Bills, minutes and memoranda on establishment and organization matters, precedents, general questions of administration and correspondence with the Treasury. Some volumes relate to specific subjects, particularly plague, but also anthrax, cholera, leprosy, smallpox, yellow fever, quarantine and emigration. The records are arranged by names of corresponding departments. Registers of correspondence are in MH 20.

MH 19/9 contains LGB copies of enclosures and reports regarding emigration of pauper children to Canada, 1887–1892. Within this document, there are detailed reports on pauper child emigrants resident in Canada between 1887–1892. The reports, compiled by the Secretary Department of Agriculture on instruction from the Dominion of Canada Immigration Officer give comments about their condition, health, character, schooling, frequency of church attendance and on each child's view of their new homes. The reports cite the Union or parish from which they were sent, as

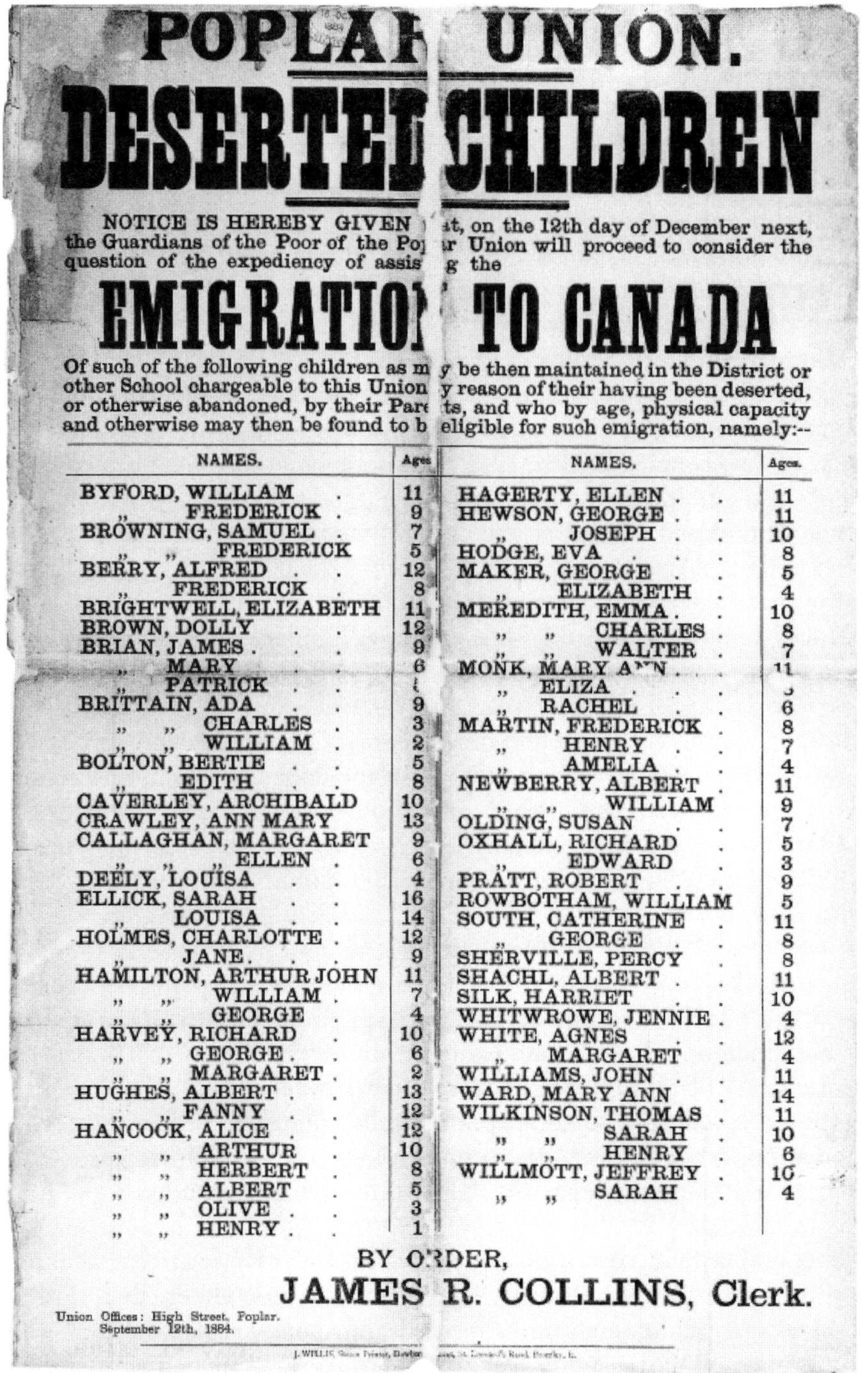

# POPLAR UNION.

# DESERTED CHILDREN

NOTICE IS HEREBY GIVEN that, on the 12th day of December next, the Guardians of the Poor of the Poplar Union will proceed to consider the question of the expediency of assisting the

# EMIGRATION TO CANADA

Of such of the following children as may be then maintained in the District or other School chargeable to this Union by reason of their having been deserted, or otherwise abandoned, by their Parents, and who by age, physical capacity and otherwise may then be found to be eligible for such emigration, namely:--

| NAMES. | Ages | NAMES. | Ages |
|---|---|---|---|
| BYFORD, WILLIAM | 11 | HAGERTY, ELLEN | 11 |
| „   FREDERICK | 9 | HEWSON, GEORGE | 11 |
| BROWNING, SAMUEL | 7 | „   JOSEPH | 10 |
| „   FREDERICK | 5 | HODGE, EVA | 8 |
| BERRY, ALFRED | 12 | MAKER, GEORGE | 5 |
| „   FREDERICK | 8 | „   ELIZABETH | 4 |
| BRIGHTWELL, ELIZABETH | 11 | MEREDITH, EMMA | 10 |
| BROWN, DOLLY | 12 | „   „   CHARLES | 8 |
| BRIAN, JAMES | 9 | „   „   WALTER | 7 |
| „   MARY | 6 | MONK, MARY ANN | 11 |
| „   PATRICK | 4 | „   ELIZA | 9 |
| BRITTAIN, ADA | 9 | „   RACHEL | 6 |
| „   „   CHARLES | 3 | MARTIN, FREDERICK | 8 |
| „   „   WILLIAM | 2 | „   HENRY | 7 |
| BOLTON, BERTIE | 5 | „   AMELIA | 4 |
| „   EDITH | 8 | NEWBERRY, ALBERT | 11 |
| CAVERLEY, ARCHIBALD | 10 | „   WILLIAM | 9 |
| CRAWLEY, ANN MARY | 13 | OLDING, SUSAN | 7 |
| CALLAGHAN, MARGARET | 9 | OXHALL, RICHARD | 5 |
| „   ELLEN | 6 | „   EDWARD | 3 |
| DEELY, LOUISA | 4 | PRATT, ROBERT | 9 |
| ELLICK, SARAH | 16 | ROWBOTHAM, WILLIAM | 5 |
| „   LOUISA | 14 | SOUTH, CATHERINE | 11 |
| HOLMES, CHARLOTTE | 12 | „   GEORGE | 8 |
| „   JANE | 9 | SHERVILLE, PERCY | 8 |
| HAMILTON, ARTHUR JOHN | 11 | SHACHL, ALBERT | 11 |
| „   „   WILLIAM | 7 | SILK, HARRIET | 10 |
| „   „   GEORGE | 4 | WHITWROWE, JENNIE | 4 |
| HARVEY, RICHARD | 10 | WHITE, AGNES | 12 |
| „   „   GEORGE | 6 | „   MARGARET | 4 |
| „   „   MARGARET | 2 | WILLIAMS, JOHN | 11 |
| HUGHES, ALBERT | 13 | WARD, MARY ANN | 14 |
| „   „   FANNY | 12 | WILKINSON, THOMAS | 11 |
| HANCOCK, ALICE | 12 | „   „   SARAH | 10 |
| „   „   ARTHUR | 10 | „   „   HENRY | 6 |
| „   „   HERBERT | 8 | WILLMOTT, JEFFREY | 10 |
| „   „   ALBERT | 5 | „   „   SARAH | 4 |
| „   „   OLIVE | 3 |  |  |
| „   „   HENRY | 1 |  |  |

BY ORDER,

## JAMES R. COLLINS, Clerk.

Union Offices: High Street, Poplar.
September 12th, 1884.

J. WILLIS, Steam Printer, Bow.

**Figure 20** Poor Law Union Papers: Poplar, London, a bill poster listing the names and ages of the children who had assisted emigration passages to Canada in September 1884 (MH 12/7698)

well as each child's name, age and host's name and address. Further Canadian government inspectors' reports and statistical information regarding child emigrants can be found in Parliamentary Papers, available on microfiche in the microfilm reading room.

Many other records of child emigration to Canada, including some Dr Barnardo archives, may now be found at the National Archives of Canada, 395 Wellington, Ottawa, Canada.

### 3.1.5 Children's Overseas Reception Board, 1940–44 (DO 131)

In May 1940 the growing menace to the UK, from both invasion and mass air attack, led to spontaneous offers of hospitality for British children from the Dominions and the USA. Offers were received through the Canadian Government and on the 31 May from private homes in Canada. In a few days, similar offers were received from Australia, New Zealand, South Africa and the USA.

On 7 June 1940 the Children's Overseas Reception Board (CORB) was set up to deal with these offers. It took the form of an Inter-Departmental Committee under the Chairmanship of Geoffrey Shakespeare MP, Parliamentary Under Secretary of State to the Dominions Office. The committee was appointed jointly by the Secretary of State for the Dominions and the Minister of Health, and was formed of representatives from the Home Office, Foreign Office, Ministry of Pensions, Scottish Office, Ministry of Health, Board of Education, Ministry of Shipping, Ministry of Labour, the Treasury and the Dominions Office. Its terms of reference were:

> To consider offers from overseas to house and care for children, whether accompanied or unaccompanied, from the European war zone, residing in Great Britain, including children orphaned by the war and to make recommendations thereon.

An Advisory Council consisting of representatives of various societies interested in migration and youth organizations was also appointed by the Chairman of the Board to advise him on the various aspects of selection, welfare and reception overseas.

A special Board for Scotland with its own Advisory Council was also set up. It followed the policy laid down by the Board in London, and a Scottish Liaison Officer was appointed to keep the Scottish Board informed of the daily decisions and progress.

These boards and advisory councils and their staff, with the help of Local Authorities, were responsible for dealing with applications, sorting, selecting and approving the

**Figure 21** Carrying of Children's Overseas Reception Board (CORB) child evacuees to New Zealand, 1940–41 (DO 131/15)

children, contacting the parents, arranging parties of children for sailing, providing escorts, collecting the children at the ports, seeing them off, and also corresponding with the Dominions authorities about reception and care overseas and the eventual return of the children after the war. The boards, and their advisory councils, were disbanded in 1944 once the perceived threat from German military activity had diminished.

Prior to the setting up of CORB, some 11,000 children had been evacuated overseas via private schemes. A total of 3,100 children were sent to Australia, Canada, New Zealand and South Africa under the CORB scheme between July and September 1940. Evacuation ceased on 17 September 1940 when the vessel SS *City of Benares* was torpedoed with the loss of 77 Canada-bound children on board. All future CORB sailings were cancelled even though the Board remained active until its disbandment four years later. Many CORB children returned to the UK after the end of hostilities to be reunited with their families.

The records in this series in the PRO consist of administrative files, a selection of case files relating to children (DO 131/94–105) and their escorts (DO 131/71–87) and registers of child applicants (DO 131/106–113). The majority of these files were destroyed under statute in 1959. Dominions Office policy files relating to the activities of the Board are in DO 35.

Contemporary newspapers in the destination countries are a source of comments and photographs, especially concerning the arrival of evacuees in the Summer of 1940.

### 3.1.6 Passenger Lists

Emigrating children are included in the PRO series of records BT 27: Outwards Passenger Lists for the period 1890–1960. Information from these records includes name of child, age, address in UK and country of origin. The records are arranged chronologically and by UK port of departure. For further information, *see* 1.3.

## 3.2 Personal records held overseas

### 3.2.1 Child emigration to Australia

Between 1947 and 1953 over 3,100 children from the UK emigrated to Australia under approved child emigration schemes. Other European countries were asked if they would like to participate in the child emigration scheme but only the UK and Malta accepted.

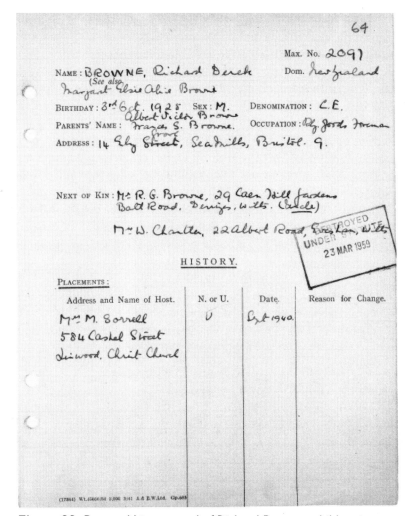

**Figure 22** Personal history card of Richard Browne, child emigrant to New Zealand (DO 131/111 p. 64)

Over 30 homes were approved by the Commonwealth for the housing of child emigrants. Most of these were run by voluntary and religious organizations. It was not government policy to provide homes specifically for emigrant children; however, the Australian government did contribute towards the capital expenditure incurred by these organizations in setting up suitable homes. Both the Commonwealth and State governments in Australia contributed towards running costs. The governments of the United Kingdom and Malta also paid maintenance for their children who had emigrated to approved institutions in Australia.

Children constituted a particularly attractive category of emigrant because they were seen to assimilate more easily, were more adaptable, had a long working life ahead and could be cheaply housed in dormitory-style accommodation.

As the role of the Commonwealth Government was mainly that of an overseer (the programmes being administered by the states), most of the records held by the National Archives of Australia are general policy files. Some series of child emigrant case files are held by a number of Australian state archives.

The Commonwealth Department of Immigration was responsible for approving the entry of individuals and recording their arrival. Matters such as accommodation, welfare and reception arrangements generally lay with state governments or charitable bodies such as the Big Brother Movement, Dr Barnardo's Homes, Fairbridge Farm Schools or institutions run by religious orders.

Records relating to child immigrants – including immigrant selection documents, passenger lists and immigration policy files – are held by the various state archives, such as the National Archives in Sydney, 120 Miller Road, Chester Hill, NSW 2162; the National Archives in Canberra, Queen Victoria Terrace, Parkes, ACT 2600; and the Melbourne Archives Centre, Casselden Place, 2 Lonsdale Street, Melbourne, VIC 3000.

### 3.2.1.1 Migrant selection documents

The range of papers usually found in the files identified as migrant selection documents includes application forms, medical reports, and other papers completed by applicants for assisted migration to Australia from Britain. Consolidated, they contain a wide range of personal details. From November 1948, papers were arranged chronologically by arrival date of the vessel or aircraft. For example, personal documents of British migrants and British assisted-passage migrants, which include children, are held from 1947 to 1968 in collections at Sydney.

### 3.2.1.2 Passenger lists

Passenger records, which include passenger lists and passenger cards, provide a rich source of family history information. Each vessel arriving at the Australian ports was required to lodge a list of incoming passengers. Arranged by date and port of arrival, passenger lists include the name of each passenger and, in earlier lists, details such as age or marital status. There are no name indexes to these records so, unless date and port of arrival are known, a search is likely to be time-consuming with no guarantee of success. Passenger lists survive for all Australian ports from 1924, with some gaps. Microfilm copies of these records are available for the years July 1924 to June 1936. Passenger lists will often need to be consulted to establish the ship's name and date of arrival, needed to access the migrant selection documents.

### 3.2.1.3 Immigration policy files

Files referring to child migration will be found in the main correspondence series of the Department of Immigration in Sydney, and some will contain information about individual children. Records are often arranged by the name of the sending agency, such as Dr Barnardo's Home.

### 3.2.1.4 Collections in other institutions

Relevant records on child migration may be held by the state government archives institutions. The Child Migrants' Trust can assist in tracing the background and families of children who came to Australia as unaccompanied child migrants. Its address is the Child Migrants' Trust, 228 Canning Street, North Carlton, VIC 3054. In addition, the Western Australia Referral Index contains basic information about child migrants to Australia between 1913 and 1968. It can be accessed through various agencies, including those marked with an asterisk below. Other sources include:

Barnardo's Australia, Head Office, 60–64 Bay Street, Ultimo, New South Wales 2007, Australia.
Catholic Migrant Centre*, 25 Victoria Square, Perth, Western Australia 6000.
C-BERS Services*, PO Box 1172, Subiaco, Western Australia 6904.
The Department of Family and Children's Services*, 189 Royal Street, East Perth, Western Australia 6004.
Poor Sisters of Nazareth, PO Box 3247, Bluff Point, Geraldton, Western Australia 6530.
Sisters of Mercy – Adelaide, Congregational Church, 34 Angus Street, Adelaide, South Australia 5000.
Sisters of St Joseph, PO Box 1150, Burwood North, New South Wales, Australia.

## 3.2.2 Child emigration to Canada

Between 1869 and the early 1930s, over 100,000 children were sent to Canada from Great Britain during the child emigration movement. Members of the British Isles Family History Society of Greater Ottawa are locating and indexing the names of these Home Children found in passenger lists in the custody of the National Archives of Canada. The database is searchable via the National Archives of Canada web site at www.archives.ca.

Also *see* http://freepages.genealogy.rootsweb.com/~britishhomechildren, the essential site for researching the British 'Home Children' who were sent to Canada between 1870 and 1940.

# 4 Prisoners Transported Overseas

Transportation was a system that exiled convicts to certain British colonies for a period of years during which time the convict would be forced to work productively and thereby learn new habits of industry and self-discipline and at the same time benefit the development of the colonial economy. Transportation, for the home government, was not a question of simply dumping human refuse on the colonies: it was genuinely thought to be effective, efficient and humane. Those who were transported were often quite young: it was after all the young who were most likely to benefit from a new life in a new world, and who were most likely to be fit enough to supply the productive labour that the new world needed. The colonial authorities, not unnaturally, tended to take a more jaundiced view of the benefits of transportation, and bitterly resented it.

After 1615, as a result of an order by the Privy Council, it became increasingly common for a pardon to be offered to convicts who had been sentenced to death on condition of transportation overseas. In 1718 an Act of Parliament (4 Geo. I c.11) standardized transportation to America at 14 years for those who had been sentenced to death and introduced a new penalty – transportation for seven years – as a sentence in its own right for a range of non-capital offences. Transportation to America ceased in 1776 because of the outbreak of the American War of Independence. It was reinstated in 1787 to Australia and Tasmania (from 1803) until 1857 when it was effectively abolished, though the Home Secretary retained the right to impose transportation for specific offences until 1868.

## 4.1 Transportation to America and the West Indies, 1615–1776

It is estimated that some 50,000 men, women and children were transported to America and the West Indies between 1614 and 1775. Most were from the poorest class and nearly half were sentenced from courts in or around London. It should be noted that transportation to the West Indies was generally for no more than ten years as most of the islands forbade longer sentences. Although the majority of cases of transportation to the West Indies took place during the period 1615–1660, between 1824 and 1853 some 9,000 convicts were sent from Britain to help build the naval and military station at Ireland Island, Bermuda.

### 4.1.1  Printed sources

Much information relating to transportation to America and the West Indies has been printed. Probably the most concise book is P W Coldham, *The Complete Book of Emigrants, 1607–1776* (Genealogical Publishing Co., 1988) which, using central and local sources, lists names of those transported together with the month and year of sentence which can provide adequate reference to the court records themselves. Other information provided is occupation, month of embarkation and landing, name of ship and destination.

The main original sources held in the PRO for transportation to America are Chancery records and Treasury records.

### 4.1.2  Trial records

Convicts transported between 1615 and 1718, or transported for 14 years after 1718 would have been convicted in a court of assizes or one with equivalent legal power. Surviving assize court records are normally held at the PRO (*see* Legal Records Information leaflets 13 and 14 which will identify the relevant record series). Convicts may have been tried in the assize or equivalent courts or at the Quarter Sessions, the records of which are held in local record offices. It should be noted that not all those who were sentenced to transportation actually went. Some convicts were successful in an application for mercy. Before 1784 reference to such applications may be found among State Papers (SP), Domestic records. *The Calendars of Home Office Papers, George III, 1760–1775*, in the Map and Large Document Room include lists of criminals with information relating to the crime committed, sentence passed, and the date and location of criminal trial. Original records to which the calendars refer are in SP 44: State Papers: Entry Books, 1661–1828.

Trial records do not usually contain useful genealogical information; nor do they contain transcripts of evidence. They may contain copies of pre-trial witness statements. The indictments were written in Latin, and in a distinctive legal handwriting, until 1733. Pre-trial witness statements are in the ordinary hand of the day, but if you are not familiar with seventeenth-century handwriting you may find it difficult to read. Sometimes reports of trials were published: the Old Bailey Proceedings, for example, were published from the 1690s onwards, and are available on microfilm for the period 1714–1834 at many large libraries (but not, as yet, in the PRO). Transcripts and pamphlets about trials in other parts of England and Wales can be traced using the *Eighteenth Century Short Title Catalogue* which is compiled by the British Library. This should be available to you at a large local reference library. A copy is available in the PRO Library.

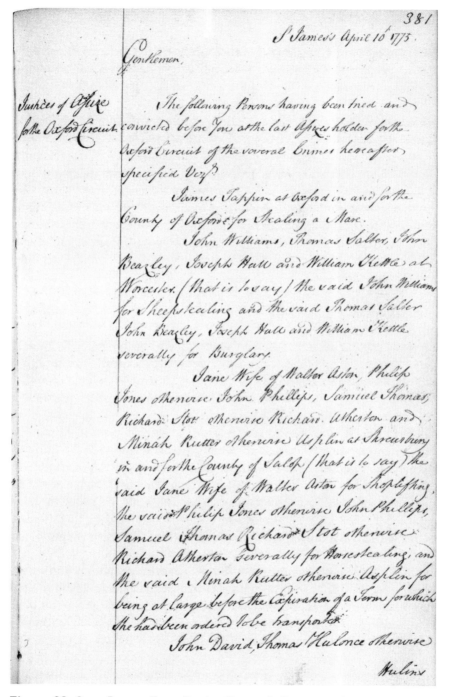

**Figure 23** State Papers, Entry Books: Criminal: Correspondence and Warrants, Pitt, Egremont, Halifax, Conway and Shelburne: Commutation of sentence of death to that of seven years' transportation for James Lappin, convicted of horse stealing, April 1775 (SP 44/91 pp. 381–3)

### 4.1.3 Pardons, appeals and petitions

C 66: Chancery and Supreme Court of Judicature: written in Latin, these parchment rolls contain a complete series of pardons from the death penalty on condition of transportation from 1654 to 1717.

SP 35: Secretaries of State: State Papers Domestic, George I and SP 36: Secretaries of State: State Papers Domestic, George II series of records contain a large and miscellaneous collection of papers concerning transportation to America. Included here are letters of appeal from convicted prisoners, their friends and families, lists of reprieved felons, and opinions of judges. *Calendars of Home Office Papers, George III, 1760–1775*, in the Map and Large Document Room, include lists of criminals with information relating to the crime committed, the date and location of criminal trial and the sentence passed. *Calendars of State Papers, Colonial, America and West Indies, 1574–1738* are available in the Research Enquiries Room. A CD-ROM version is also available in the PRO Library.

### 4.1.4 Transportation lists

T 1: Treasury Papers series includes a mass of transportation lists starting in 1747 and ending in 1772. *Calendars of Treasury Papers, 1557–1728, Treasury Books, 1600–1718,* and *Treasury Books and Papers, 1729–1745* are available in the Research Enquiries Room.

T 53: Treasury: Entry Books of Warrants relating to the Payment of Money includes records of payment made by the Treasury to contractors engaged in the transportation of felons between 1718 and 1752. Until 1744 the names of all those to be transported from the City of London and the Home Counties, together with the names of the ships in which they were to be transported, and the destination American colony, are included in the Money Books. Thereafter, only statistics concerning transported felons are entered, together with the names of the transporting ships and their masters.

CO 5: Board of Trade and Secretaries of State: America and West Indies, Original Correspondence, 1606–1822, includes material on all aspects relating to transportation to America and the West Indies. A key finding aid to this series is *Calendars of State Papers, Colonial, America and West Indies, 1574–1738*, available in the Research Enquiries Room. A CD-ROM version is also available in the PRO Library.

## 4.2 Transportation to Australia, 1787–1868

Following the outbreak of the American Revolution in 1776, America ceased to be an option for transporting criminals. Sentences of transportation were still passed, but convicts were held in prison instead. Naturally these soon became overcrowded, and extra accommodation had to be provided in old ships (the 'hulks') moored in coastal waters (*see* 4.2.4). The solution to the crisis was to develop a new penal colony and in 1787 the First Fleet of 11 ships set sail to establish a new penal colony at Botany Bay on the east coast of Australia. A second fleet followed in 1790 and a third left in 1791.

It is estimated that over 1,000 ships transported in excess of 165,000 men, women and children to Australia (New South Wales) and Tasmania (Van Diemen's land) between 1787 and 1867. In the 1830s 4,000 people were being transported every year. Also, from 1850 to 1868 it is estimated that a further 9,500 male convicts were transported to Western Australia.

Transportation was not formally abolished until 1868, but in practice it was effectively stopped in 1857, and had become increasingly unusual well before that date.

Records of convicts transported from Ireland, 1791–1853, are available at the National Archives of Ireland. They include Prisoners' Petitions and Cases 1788–1836 and transportation Registers, 1836–1857. They can be accessed by name of convict at www.nationalarchives.ie/search01.html.

### 4.2.1 Printed sources

There is no single index to the names of those transported to Australia. To find out more about a convict you will need to have a good idea of when they were tried and/or the date of transportation and ship in which he or she sailed to Australia.

Much information relating to transportation to Australia has been printed. Details of convicts who sailed on the early fleets have been published in books such as P G Fidlon and R J Ryan (eds) *1788: The First Fleeters* (Australian Documents Library, 1981), D Chapman, *People of the First Fleet* (Cassell, 1981), M Gillen, *The Founders of Australia: A Biographical Dictionary of the First Fleet* (Library of Australian History, 1989), M Flynn, *The Second Fleet: Britain's grim convict armada of 1790* (Library of Australian History, 1989), and R J Ryan, *The Third Fleeters*, (Horwitz Grahame, 1983).

For later years, names of convicts and settlers appear on the published censuses for the penal colonies, the most complete being the Census of New South Wales in November 1828. Edited by M R Sainty and K A Johnson, this census was published in

1980 by the Library of Australian History. The original records of the 1828 census are available on microfilm at the PRO in the series HO 10 (*see* 5.2.6).

Details of convicts may also be found on the microfiche index to the New South Wales Convict Indents and Ships. Compiled by the Genealogical Society of Victoria, the index records the names and aliases of some 124,000 convicts who arrived in New South Wales and Van Dieman's Land between 1788 and 1842, when transportation to New South Wales effectively ended. The index is almost wholly based on the Ships' Indents (Indentures) which are the documents recording the formal transfer of prisoners to the Governor of the colony receiving them. Each entry in the index (available in the Microfilm Reading Room) records the name or alias of convict, the name of the ship and its arrival date, and a reference to the relevant page(s) on the Indent(s) that have been reproduced on microfiche by State Records New South Wales as part of their Genealogical Research Kit. The fiche collection also includes an index of ships that transported the convicts. It shows the arrival date for each voyage together with the particular fiche and film that contains the records. A CD-ROM version of these indexes is available in the PRO Library.

All the above sources are available at the PRO and the Society of Genealogists.

The Genealogical Society of Victoria have catalogues relating to the 80,000 convicts transported to New South Wales between 1788 and 1849, 70,000 bound for Tasmania (1803–1853), and 10,000 male convicts transported to Western Australia (1850–1853). Catalogues include records relating to convict arrivals, musters and papers, assignment registers, registers of tickets of leave, registers of pardons, applications for marriage and convict death returns. The records here also provide details of convicts' children in Tasmania, many of whom arrived with their convict parent or parents and were unnamed on the convict lists. The records comprise information relating to destitute children and refer to the setting up of an orphanage by Governor Arthur, in 1825, to house the many destitute children.

Useful web sites for Australian convicts include: http://members.iinet.net.au/ ~reginald/convicts.htm#references. This provides full lists of convicts transported to Western Australia between 1850 and 1887 giving details of offences. Sources used in compiling this useful web site include original archives held in Australia and the UK.

### 4.2.2  Trial records

Surviving records of assize trials are held in the PRO. The assize records are not indexed by personal name: instead, they are arranged by assize circuit, and then by record type. To find a particular case, you must know the name of the accused, the county or circuit where he or she was tried and the approximate date of the trial. For the nineteenth century, if you do not know where or when the accused was tried, you can look at the Annual Criminal Registers, for England and Wales 1805–1892 in HO 27 or in HO 26, Criminal Registers, for Middlesex, 1791–1849. Available on microfiche in the Microfilm Reading Room is an index to HO 27, arranged by county and then by name within.

Both series list those charged with indictable offences, giving place of trial, verdict and sentence. Once you have a reference to a date and place of trial, check the various series of records for criminal assizes held in English and Welsh assizes (these are listed in the following legal records information series: no.14, English Assizes: Key for Criminal Trials, 1559–1971, and no.15, Welsh Assizes, 1831–1971: Key to Classes for Criminal and Civil Trials. Survival of assize records is patchy, as the clerks of assize, who kept them, tended to destroy them when their bulk became too much. If a suitable record exists for the year and place in question, go to the series list of the series indicated. Records of trials at courts of quarter sessions are *not* in the PRO, but at local record offices.

Criminal trial records are very formal; they do not normally contain either transcripts of evidence or any information about age and family relationships. In addition, the information given about occupation and residence is rarely accurate.

### 4.2.3 Pardons, appeals and petitions

If you really want good quality personal information about a convict, then you would be better advised to look for an application for clemency. Because people asking for clemency or a pardon wanted to prove that they were worthy of mercy, they often include a lot of information designed to establish how respectable they were and this would include just the kind of details about personal circumstances and family background that family historians want to know.

HO 17: Criminal Petitions, Series I, 1819–1839 and HO 18: Home Office: Criminal Petitions, Series II, 1839–1854, are arranged in coded bundles so you will need to use the registers in HO 19 to identify the right one. The registers are arranged by the date of receipt of the petition. They date back to 1797 and include information about the response to the petition, so you can sometimes find out something useful about a convict even if the petition itself does not survive.

There are also petitions in HO 48: Law Officers' Reports, Opinions and Correspondence, 1782–1871; HO 49: Law Officers' Letter Books, 1762–1871; HO 54: Civil Petitions and Addresses, 1783–1854; and HO 56: Petitions Entry Books, 1784–1922. These records, however, are not indexed.

HO 47: Judges' Reports on Criminals, 1784–1829 and HO 6: Judges' and Recorders' Returns, 1816–1840, are also informative. They sometimes include an unofficial transcript of evidence (together with comments on the characters of both witnesses and juries) as well as memorials and petitions from friends and relatives of the accused. The *Calendars of Home Office Papers, George III, 1760–1775*, in the Map and Large Document Room also include Judges' Reports on Criminals.

It was possible for wives to accompany their convict husbands, and some wives applied to do so. Their petitions survive in PC 1: Privy Council and Privy Council Office: Miscellaneous Unbound Papers, notably PC 1/67–92 for 1819–1844 and for 1849–1871 in HO 12: Criminal Department: Old Criminal (OC) Papers. HO 12 references can be identified via HO 14: Criminal Department: Registers of Papers, 1849–1870. CO 201: New South Wales Original Correspondence, 1783–1900, and CO 386: Colonial Office: Land and Emigration Commission, etc., 1833–1894, includes letters from people wishing to join convict relatives. For example, CO 386/154 consists of a register of applications for passages to the colonies for convicts' families, 1848–1873.

### 4.2.4 Transportation lists

HO 11: Convict Transportation, 1787–1870 provides the name of the ship on which the convict sailed as well as the date and place of conviction and the term of the sentence. They are not indexed by name of convict, but if you know the name of the ship and preferably also when it either left England or arrived in Australia, it should be relatively easy to find the convict. There is a card index to convict ships in the Research Enquiries Room. It refers to records in HO 11 and ADM 101: Office of the Director General of the Medical Department of the Navy and predecessors: Medical Journals, 1785–1963. ADM 101 includes journals from convict ships and emigrant ships (1817–1856), for which naval surgeons were provided. The journals contain an account of the treatment of medical and surgical cases, and usually a copy of the daily sick list, statistical abstracts of the incidence of diseases, and general comments on the health and activities of the ship's company. Similar journals can be found in MT 32: Admiralty Transport Department, Surgeon Superintendents' Journals of Convict Ships, 1858–1867.

PC 1: Privy Council and Privy Council Office: Miscellaneous Unbound Papers, 1481–1946, and PC 2: Privy Council: Registers, 1540–1978 contains additional material about transportation. The registers, for example, give lists of convicts transported for 14 years or less. TS 18: Treasury Solicitor: General Series Papers, 1517–1923, includes contracts with agents to transport the prisoners, with full lists of ships and convicts, 1842–1867, in TS 18/460–525 and 1308–1361.

After America no longer became an option for transporting criminals in 1776, sentences of transportation were still passed, but convicts were held in prison instead.

As these became overcrowded, extra accommodation had to be provided in old ships (the 'hulks') moored in coastal waters and these held many of those who were included on the First Fleet to Australia in 1787.

Records of those awaiting transportation in prison hulks (ship prisons) are also available at the PRO. HO 8: Home Office: Convict Prisons: Quarterly Returns of Prisoners, 1824–1876 consist of sworn lists of convicts on board the hulks and in convict prisons with particulars as to their ages, convictions and sentences, health and behaviour.

## 4.2.5 Settlement in Australia

As mentioned in 4.2.1, much has been published relating to convict settlement in Australia, including many of the censuses and musters, such as many of the records in HO 10: Settlers and Convicts, New South Wales and Tasmania: Records, 1787–1859. The New South Wales census of 1828 (HO 10/21–27) is the most complete, and is available in a published edition by Sainty and Johnson. It contains the names of more than 35,000 people with details of age, religion, family, place of residence, occupation and stock or land held. Whether each settler came free, or as a convict (or was born in the colony) is recorded; and date of arrival and the name of the ship are given. The musters or similar material for New South Wales and Norfolk Island, 1800–1802, for New South Wales, Norfolk Island and Van Diemen's Land (Tasmania), 1811, and for New South Wales in 1822 and 1837 have also been published and are available at the PRO (details are given in the Bibliography).

Similar material can be found in CO 201: Colonial Office and Predecessors: New South Wales Original Correspondence, 1783–1900. These include the victualling lists for Norfolk Island, an island 1670 kilometres north-east off the east Sydney coast of Australia. Papers relating to convicts in New South Wales and Tasmania in HO 10 contain material about convicts' pardons and tickets of leave from New South Wales and Tasmania, 1835–59. HO 7: Convicts, Miscellanea, 1785–1835 include, in HO 7/2, information about deaths of convicts in New South Wales, 1829–1834.

Lists of convicts, together with emigrants, 1801–1821, who settled in Australia can be found in CO 201. Names can also be traced in CO 202: New South Wales Entry Books, 1786–1823, CO 360: New South Wales Register of Correspondence, 1849–1900, and CO 369: New South Wales Register of Out-Letters, 1873–1900. Records of the superintendent of convicts in New South Wales, 1788–1825, are held in the State Archives of New South Wales; the PRO holds microfilm copies in CO 207. Some of the lists from these records have been printed in L L Robson, *The Convict Settlers of Australia*.

# 5 Life-Cycle Records of the British Overseas

For whatever reason, hundreds of thousands of British citizens have emigrated or lived overseas throughout the centuries and for the latter part of that time information related to their birth, marriage or death overseas can be traced among records found in a number of UK archives. Unfortunately, there is no centralized collection of such records. The FRC holds a large collection of these records relating mainly to English and Welsh citizens in countries that were not colonies. The Scottish and Irish General Register Offices hold similar records for Scottish and Irish emigrants. The PRO holds life-cycle records of Britons abroad, relating mostly to foreign countries but also some colonies. In some cases, copies of FRC records are held at Kew and vice versa.

## 5.1 FRC sources

### 5.1.1 ONS Registers

The Overseas Section at the FRC holds the following statutory records relating to births, marriages and deaths of Britons overseas:

- Births and deaths at sea (marine) registered from July 1837;
- Regimental (1761–1924), army chaplains' returns and Service Departmental registers of births, deaths and marriages (from 1796);
- RAF returns of births, marriages and deaths from 1920 (with army returns to 1950 for deaths, to 1955 for births, to 1949 for marriages, and then in Service Department indexes);
- Royal Naval returns of births, marriages and deaths from 1959;
- Consular returns of births, marriages and deaths for British citizens abroad from July 1849;
- Civilian aviation births and deaths and missing (presumed dead) from 1947;
- High Commission returns of births and deaths from the date of the independence of the Commonwealth country onwards;
- Military and civil registers, Chaplain's Register Ionian Islands, births, marriages and deaths, 1818–1864;
- War deaths: Natal and South Africa Forces, Boer War (1899–1902);
- First World War (1914–1921) – Army officers, other ranks (including RAF); Naval, all ranks (including RAF); Indian services war deaths (1914–1921);
- Second World War (3 September 1939–30 June 1948) – Army officers, other ranks; Naval officers, ratings; Royal Air Force, all ranks; Indian Services war deaths (1939–1948).

In most cases the records extend up to 1965 as separate registers. Thereafter, there are single annual series for all births, deaths and marriages of British subjects overseas. The references within these index volumes can enable the certificate to be ordered. These will provide further information relating to the birth, death or marriage, similar to that available for those registered in England and Wales (*see* Stella Colwell, *The Family Records Centre: a user's guide*, PRO Publications, 2002). Postal applications can be processed at the Office of National Statistics, Certificate Enquiries, PO Box 2, Southport, Merseyside PR8 2JD, Tel: 0151 471 4816.

Microfiche copies of all the above indexes up until 1992 are also available at Kew in the Microfilm Reading Room.

### 5.1.2 The IGI

The IGI (International Genealogical Index) is an incomplete index to births/baptisms and marriages covering most of the world, compiled by the Church of Jesus Christ of Latter Day Saints (LDS). The 1992 edition of the IGI British Isles version is available at the FRC on microfiche and is arranged alphabetically by county.

The IGI contains millions of names gathered from a number of sources all over the world. Although hundreds of millions of names have been included it is important to remember that the index is not comprehensive and is only updated every few years. At Kew, in the Microfilm Reading Room, is the IGI, British Isles version, for 1988 and 1992.

The main use of the IGI is in searching for people before 1837 when civil registration began, but it can also be useful in locating where your family lived.

The worldwide version of the IGI is also available on www.familysearch.org, a computer compilation containing millions of facts relevant to family historians. They have been collected from a variety of sources, ranging from information extracted from vital records to information given by individuals researching their own family histories. The Vital Records Index (VRI), consisting of extracted information only, and not found in the IGI, is gradually being added to www.familysearch.org. The British Isles VRI is available on CD-ROM at the FRC.

Most entries within these sources provide name, names of parents (for baptisms) or spouse (for marriages), gender, type of event – b=birth, c=christening/baptism, m=marriage, date of event and place of event.

The United States Social Security Index from about 1960 includes details which may enable you to trace migrant relatives to their state of last abode. It is available on CD-ROM at the FRC.

## 5.2 PRO sources

### 5.2.1 Registrar General returns

A miscellaneous series of returns of births, baptisms, marriages, deaths and burials of Britons at sea or abroad is held at Kew among Registrar General (RG) records. These non-statutory records, originally records of the Bishop of London, were transferred to the PRO in 1977 and are indexed (in a fashion), 1627–1960, in RG 43, which is available on microfilm both in the Microfilm Reading Room and the PRO section of the FRC.

Also available on microfilm at both sites are some of the registers to which RG 43 relates – RG 32: General Register Office: Miscellaneous Foreign Returns (1831–1968), RG 33: General Register Office: Foreign Registers and Returns (1627–1960), RG 34: General Register Office: Miscellaneous Foreign Marriage Returns (1826–1921), RG 35: General Register Office: Miscellaneous Foreign Death Returns (1830–1921) and RG 36: General Register Office: Registers and Returns of Births, Marriages and Deaths in the Protectorates etc. of Africa and Asia (1895–1965). Not all the index entries in RG 43 relate to RG 32–36. Some concern non-parochial registers and records in RG 4–8, also available at both Kew and the FRC. For example, RG 43/1 includes a few references to  births registered between 1784–1791 at Funchal, Portugal, which are relevant to Dr Williams' Library (RG 5). Reference is also made in some RG 43 indexes to service registers and other statutory registers, which remain in the custody of the Office for National Statistics and are explained in 5.1.

The RG records contain largely non-statutory records relating to births, baptisms, marriages, deaths and burials abroad, and on British as well as foreign ships, of British subjects, nationals of the colonies, the Commonwealth and countries under British jurisdiction. Events affecting some foreign nationals are also included. Records consist mainly of certificates issued by foreign registration authorities, which are in local languages, and copies of entries kept by incumbents of English churches and missions, chaplains and burial authorities. There are also documents sent by individuals to the Registrar General. For the Second World War period some notifications of deaths of members of the services, prisoners of war, civilians, internees and deaths through aircraft lost in flight are included.

The registers are subject to the 30-year closure rule, so those where the last entry in the register is 1972 should become available in 2003. Not all registers are annual so it may be longer than 30 years when information from a particular year is made available.

Also available among RG records is RG 6: Society of Friends' Registers, Notes and Certificates of Births, Marriages and Burials, 1578–1841. This series contains registers of births, deaths, burials and marriages of congregations of the Religious Society of Friends (Quakers) in England and Wales. The documents in the series are arranged by

Quarterly Meetings, which consisted of a county or combinations of counties. Many of the registers contain integral indexes, either at the front or rear of the volumes. The former reference number is the reference number allocated to the document at the time of its transfer. The 55 files of original birth and burial notes and marriage certificates consist of combinations of pre- and post-1776 originals filed chronologically, with the pre-1776 notes often in handwritten form. Quaker men's preparative meetings minutes, and those of women's meetings, include testimonials given to members leaving for new destinations. These can be linked to emigrants, and conversely the filed testimonials in North America can be used to link back to places of origin in England and Wales. These are really good sources for members of the Society of Friends. Microfilm copies of RG 6 are available on open access at both the PRO and FRC.

Generally speaking, RG registrations do not provide as much biographical information as the ONS certificates described in 5.1.

## 5.2.2 Foreign Office records

Duplicate consular copies of birth, marriage and death registers described in 5.1 are held in Foreign Office embassy and consular office records (FO series). These include some of the duplicate registers of births, marriages and deaths from which the consuls' returns to the Registrar General were compiled. There is also a 46-volume series of consular correspondence with the Foreign Office on marriages abroad, covering 1814–1905. The series is split between FO 83 and FO 97, with a register and index for 1814–1893 at FO 802/239. It includes information on some individual marriages. Also in FO 83 are covering despatches to certificates of marriages abroad giving the names of the parties, 1846–1890; general correspondence and circulars on consular marriages; and acknowledgements of receipt of certificates by the Bishop of London's Registry.

These FO records also include a number of unique registers of baptisms and burials of British residents overseas along with registers of passports issued at consulates (*see* 1.5.2) and papers relating to the wills and estates of British expatriates.

References to twentieth-century correspondence can be traced in the Foreign Office card index for 1906–1919, and in the printed index for 1920–1951; both these indexes are in the Research Enquiries Room at Kew. However, many of the documents they refer to no longer exist. Similar records for the period before 1906 can be found using FO 566: Registers of General Correspondence, 1817–1920 and FO 605: Registers (Library Series) and Indexes of General Correspondence, 1761–1893. The registers and indexes provide a means of reference to papers for the years 1808 to 1890 contained in the volumes of general correspondence before 1906.

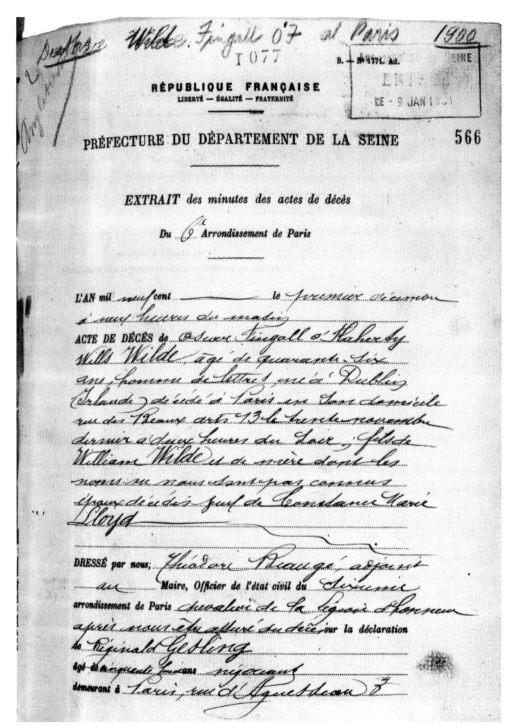

**Figure 24** Miscellaneous Foreign Deaths, death certificate of Oscar Wilde (RG 35/35, p. 1077)

### 5.2.3 Merchant shipping registers

Following the Merchant Shipping Act 1854, registers were compiled, from ships' official logs, of births, deaths and marriages of passengers at sea.

Births, marriages and deaths are all recorded from 1854–1883, births and deaths only from 1883–1887 and deaths only from 1888 to 1890. These records are in the series BT 158: Registers of Births, Deaths and Marriages of Passengers at Sea. Masters were further required by the Registration of Births and Deaths Act 1874 to report births and deaths of both United Kingdom subjects and aliens to the Registrar General of Shipping: the information about United Kingdom subjects is in the series BT 160: Registers of Births of British Nationals at Sea and BT 159: Registers of Deaths of British Nationals at Sea. Records of births and deaths at sea, 1891–1964, are held in BT 334 with a marriage register for 1854–1972. Also *see* 1.2.5.

Details of some births and baptisms at sea (potentially from 1831 and 1931) are also included in Registrar General registers (*see* 5.2.1), particularly RG 32/1–16 (indexed in RG 43/2). Also among these records can be found registers of marriages aboard naval ships, 1842–1889 (RG 33/156, indexed in RG 43/7).

Registers of the deaths of emigrants at sea, 1847–1869, can also be found among Colonial Office records in CO 386/169–172. CUST 67/74 consists of a register of deaths and births at sea, 1892–1918, for the Customs outport of Falmouth.

Registers of deaths of merchant seamen are discussed in 5.2.4.2.

### 5.2.4 Military returns

Although most military overseas registers can be found among ONS records described in 5.1, some original registers can also be found at the PRO.

#### 5.2.4.1 Army records

The PRO has a small number of regimental registers of births, baptisms, marriages and burials, of the kind kept by the FRC (ONS). Some of these are annotated with information on discharge: others have the baptismal entries of the children entered on the same page as the marriage certificate of the parents.

The PRO has baptism and marriage registers for the following:

| Regiment | Former militia name | Dates | PRO references |
|---|---|---|---|
| 3rd King's Own Yorkshire Light Infantry | 1st West Yorkshire Militia | 1865–1904 | WO 68/499 |
| Rifle Brigade, 6th battalion Royal Horse Artillery | 114th Westmeath Militia | 1834–1904 1817–1827, 1859–1883 (most are 1860–1877) | WO 68/439 WO 69/63–73, WO 69/551–582 |
| Somerset Light Infantry, 3rd and 4th battalions | Somerset Militia | 1836–1887, 1892–1903 | WO 68/441 |
| West Norfolk Regiment | | 1863–1908 | WO 68/497 |
| West Yorkshire Rifles, 3rd battalion | 2nd West Yorkshire Militia | 1832–1877 | WO 68/499 |

In addition, there are baptisms and banns of marriage for Army personnel in Palestine, 1939–1947 in WO 156, *see also* 2.7.2.1.

From about 1868 to about 1883, at the end of each muster (or at the beginning for regiments stationed in India), may be found a marriage roll, which lists wives and children for whom married quarters were provided. The main series of muster books and pay lists in WO 12 and WO 16 are arranged by regiment, though separate series survive for the Royal Artillery (WO 10), Royal Engineers (WO 11), and Militia and Volunteers (WO 13). The quarterly muster books normally note where the regiment or unit was located, record the names of officers and men and their rank, pay and enlistment date. They also list ages of recruits, their non-effectives. Birthplaces of soldiers are normally recorded at the end of each quarterly muster. The lists of non-effectives also give dates of death and where the soldiers died in service.

Each regiment made regular returns of its casualties, where the usual round of one or two deaths from sickness is suddenly broken by long lists of men killed in action. Nominal rolls of the dead were kept for many of the campaigns fought during the second half of the nineteenth century and early twentieth century.

| China | 1857–1858 | WO 32/8221, 8224, 8227 |
| | 1860 | WO 32/8230, 8233, 8234 |
| New Zealand | 1860 | WO 32/8255 |
| | 1863–1864 | WO 32/8263–8268, 8271, 8276–8280 |
| South Africa | 1878–1881 | WO 25/3474, 7770, 7706–7708, 7727, 7819 |
| Egypt | 1882, 1884 | WO 25/3473 |
| Sudan | 1884–1885 | WO 25/3473, 6123, 6125–6126, 8382 |
| Burma | 1888 | WO 25/3473 |
| Sierra Leone | 1898 | WO 32/7630–7631 |
| South Africa | 1899–1902 | WO 108/89–91, 338 |
| China | 1915 | WO 32/4996B |

Some of these have been published: Cook and Cook's *The Casualty Roll for the Crimea*, and the *South Africa Field Force Casualty List, 1899–1902*, are available at Kew, as are microfilm and CD-ROM copies of *Soldiers who died in the Great War,* a CD-ROM copy of *Officers who died in the Great War* (the First World War) and a CD-ROM copy of *Army, Roll of Honour – World War II, Soldiers who died in the Second World War, 1939–1945.* A lot of this information is also available via the Commonwealth War Graves Commission, 2 Marlow Road, Maidenhead, Berkshire SL6 7DX, available on-line at www.cwgc.org. The on-line Debt of Honour Register (available at www.yard.ccta.gov.uk) provides personal and service details and places of commemoration for the 1.7 million members of the Commonwealth forces who died in the First or Second World Wars.

Army service records of officers in WO 25 and WO 76 for 1828–1829 and sporadic years thereafter, give details of birth, marriage and their offspring, together with details of where, normally abroad, these events occurred.

Also at the PRO among records of the Registrar General (RG), described in 5.2.1, are French and Belgian certificates of the deaths of British soldiers who died in hospitals or elsewhere outside the immediate war zone, 1914–1920. These records are arranged by surname in RG 35/45–69. Certificates for surnames beginning with the letters C, F, P, Q and X are missing. For the Second World War, there are retrospective registers of deaths from enemy action in the Far East 1941–1945 (RG 33/11 and 132, indexed in RG 43/14). The Army Roll of Honour for the Second World War is in WO 304, though much of this has been used to create the CD-ROM of *Army, Roll of Honour – World War II, Soldiers who died in the Second World War, 1939–1945.*

*See* 2.1.3 for series of War Office records relating to the settlement of soldiers overseas.

### 5.2.4.2 Royal Navy and Merchant Navy records

There is no discrete series of records relating to overseas life-cycle records of Royal Navy personnel.

ADM 121: Admiralty and Ministry of Defence: Mediterranean Station: Correspondence and Papers 1843–1968, include records of deaths and burials of Royal Navy officers and ratings at Mediterranean stations, together with records of births and baptisms of their children. Similar registers may be found in ADM 6: Admiralty: Service Records, Registers, Returns and Certificates, specifically ADM 6/436 for Ireland Island, Bermuda (burials 1848–1946) and ADM 6/439 for Boaz Garrison, Bermuda (baptisms, 1903–18).

Further information on deaths overseas of Royal Navy Officers and ratings is available at the Commonwealth War Graves Commission.

The Seamen's Fund Winding-up Act 1851 (section 29) required masters of British ships to hand on to a Shipping Master at the end of all voyages the wages and effects, or their proceeds, of any seamen who died during the voyage.

Registers of deaths of merchant seamen from 1852 to 1881 and 1888 to 1893 are in BT 153: Registers of Wages and Effects of Deceased Seamen. Registers for the period April 1881 to May 1888 have not survived. The means of reference to this series are: BT 154: Index to Seamen's Names and BT 155: Index to Ships' Names. Associated with these registers are BT 156: Monthly Lists of Deaths of Seamen, 1886 to 1889, and BT 157: Registers of Seamen's Deaths Classified by Cause, 1882 to 1889. From 1890, the Registrar General of Shipping and Seamen introduced a new series of records, which combined records of the births, deaths and marriages of passengers at sea with the records of deaths and marriages of seamen at sea. These registers are in BT 334: Registers and Indexes of Births, Marriages and Deaths of Passengers and Seamen at Sea, 1891 to 1972, and are discussed in 5.3.3.

BT 98: General Register and Record Office of Seamen: Agreements and Crew Lists, Series I, 1747–1860 and BT 99: Registrar General of Shipping and Seamen and predecessor: Agreements and Crew Lists, Series II, 1861–1990, also record deaths of Merchant Navy crew, with short reports and sale inventories of their personal effects.

Registers of payments to Navy pensioners (including some widows and orphans) at British colonies can be found in WO 22: Royal Hospital Chelsea: Pensions Returns, 1842–1883 (*see* 5.2.4.1).

BT 339: Board of Trade: Registrar General of Shipping and Seamen: Rolls of Honour, Wars of 1914–1918 and 1939–1945 contains volumes which lists the dead, and missing presumed dead, from the ranks of the merchant marine fleets during the wars of 1914–1918 and 1939–1945. BT 164/23 includes records of casualties and deaths of Royal Naval Reserve Officers, 1939–1946.

BT 341: Registrar General of Shipping and Seamen: Inquiries into Deaths at Sea: Papers and Reports, 1939–1964, contains the Registrar General of Shipping and Seamen's files on inquiries into deaths at sea. The files contain correspondence, papers and reports regarding deaths at sea in order to establish that there was sufficient information to record a death, rather than a missing presumed dead.

The dead include crew and passengers of all nationalities. The files typically include: sworn testimonies of survivors; particulars of the deceased; medical officers' and inspectors' statements; answers to medical circumstances of death; examinations on oath; Forms B and D 3 containing detailed particulars of the cause of death; Form Inq 6 Death on Board a British Foreign-Going Ship; newspaper cuttings, and particulars of death, injury, ill-treatment, punishment or casualty on or to a fishing boat.

It should be noted that not all the cases concern fatalities 'on board' ship; they can include the circumstances of deaths of passengers or seamen en route to the ship.

The information contained in the files was initially collected according to the recommendations of the Merchant Shipping Act 1894.

The files are arranged chronologically and then alphabetically by ship's name.

### 5.2.4.3 Air records

Aside from the ONS indexes to deaths of men in the air services available at the FRC and referred to under 5.1, the PRO holds French and Belgian death certificates for airmen who died in hospitals or elsewhere outside the immediate war zone in RG 35/45–69.

A roll of honour for members of the Royal Flying Corps (RFC) and Royal Naval Auxiliary Corps (RNAS) who died during the First World War is available at the Imperial War Museum, Lambeth Road, London SE1 6HZ. *The London Gazette* in ZJ 1 (available on microfilm at Kew for the period 1914–18 and 1939–45) published weekly casualty lists.

The most useful source for details of casualties are the sets of the RFC and RNAS casualty cards held by the RAF Museum. These cards include casualties on the Western Front and give information relating to reason for casualty, type of machine and sometimes next of kin. The PRO holds many lists of casualties in AIR 1/843–860,

914–916, and 960–969. Some lists of RFC officers reported missing are in AIR 1/435/ 25/273/1–4.

Information relating to the location of graves of airmen and dates of death and unit during the First World War can be obtained from the on-line Debt of Honour Register (available at www.yard.ccta.gov.uk). At the PRO, AIR 27: Operations Record Books, Squadrons, 1911–1977, include mention of deaths of flying personnel.

### 5.2.5  Colonial Office returns

CO 386: Colonial Office: Land and Emigration Commission, etc., 1833–1894, contain three registers of life-cycle records of emigrants at sea. These are: CO 386/170: Births and Deaths, 1847–1854; CO 386/171: Deaths, 1854–1860; and CO 386/172: Deaths, 1861–1869.

These registers were compiled for ships chartered by the Colonial Land and Emigration Commissioners to carry emigrants. They are primarily registers of deaths, since a bounty was paid by the Commission for emigrants landed alive. Each volume has an index of the ships included, giving the ship's name, the destination colony and the year of the voyage. The index to the earliest volume also has an occasional note of a particular class of passenger, such as convicts, pensioners or orphans. There is no name index to the emigrants referred to in these registers.

The main destination for these ships was Australia. The Cape of Good Hope has a few entries recorded throughout these years. The returns from 1859 also include reference to destinations such as India, as well as New Zealand, Tasmania, British Columbia and the Falkland Islands.

Standard information is recorded in these registers such as name, gender and age, as well as the date of death and (where known) cause of death. There is a summary total of all deaths during a given journey. The age for which most deaths are recorded is, unsurprisingly, that of children under three. Major causes of death recorded in all age groups were diarrhoea, various forms of fever, dysentery, cholera and measles. Where a death occurred in quarantine on arrival, this is recorded in the register, since the bounty could still be claimed.

The birth registers record only the numbers of births recorded on a particular voyage and no names are given. Deaths among these babies are recorded separately in the register. The later registers give the sex of the child.

Colonial Government Gazettes and Colonial Newspapers also provide information relating to life-cycle records (*see* 2.1.2).

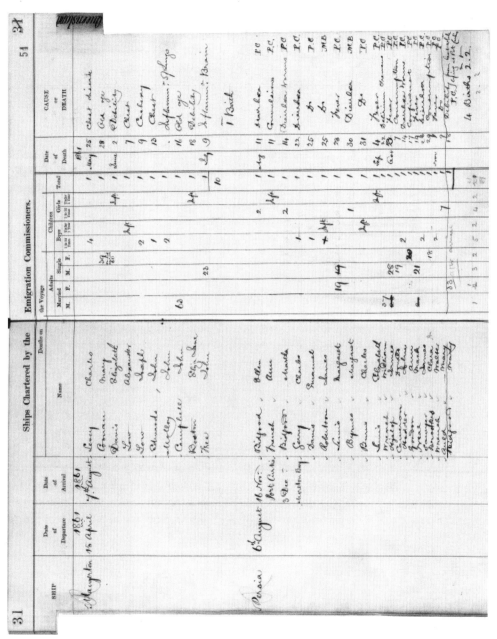

**Figure 25** Deaths of passengers at sea in 1861 (CO 386/172, fol. 54)

### 5.2.6  Census records and other listings

Regular reports relating to the colonial populations were sought from 1670 following the creation of the Council for Foreign Plantations. The information was mainly statistical and helped assist the British government in assessing the economic wealth of the colonies and their military strength. Statistical counts of population, together with other types of returns of populations such as petitions from prominent landowners, tax returns, and electoral registers, occur in the blue books of statistics and government gazettes for the individual colonies, and are occasionally printed in the British parliamentary papers, available on microfiche in the Microfilm Reading Room.

Among the more famous colonial censuses that provide personal details of inhabitants are CO 122: War and Colonial Department and Colonial Office: Heligoland, Miscellanea, and HO 10: Home Office: Settlers and Convicts, New South Wales and Tasmania: Records. Included within CO 122 is CO 122/37, a census of population in Heligoland taken in 1881 recording the names, ages, sex and professions, and, within HO 10 (available on microfilm), a census of 1828 relating to the population of New South Wales and Tasmania. This is the most complete and therefore the most valuable of all colonial censuses. It contains details of more than 35,000 persons with their ages, religions, families, residences, occupations and details of stock and land held. In addition, there is an indication of whether they were coming to the colony free or in bond, or were born in the colony, and of the ship and year of arrival. HO 10 also includes censuses in New South Wales and Tasmania for other periods between 1788 and 1859.

CO 267: Sierra Leone Original Correspondence contains a census of population and liberated Africans in 1831 in CO 267/111 and CO 267/127 and a census of white inhabitants in Barbados in 1715 can be found in CO 28/16.

G Grannum, *Tracing Your West Indian Ancestors* (PRO, 1995) provides details of Colonial Office (CO) sources relating to the West Indies. For example, there is a considerable amount of information on the inhabitants of Barbados, 1678–1680, including lists of property owners, their wives, children, servants and slaves, some parish registers, and lists of the militia (CO 1/44 no. 47 i–xxxvii, CO 29/9 pp. 1–3): there is a descriptive list of the various records (with no names) in the *Calendar of State Papers, Colonial America and West Indies, 1677–1680*, no. 1236 i–xxxvii, which should be consulted first.

Some information on colonists is contained in the correspondence and papers of the Colonial Office, which covers the West Indies as well as the continent of America, and starts in 1574: see the printed *Calendars of State Papers Colonial* which are available in the Research Enquiries Room and in the Library on CD-ROM.

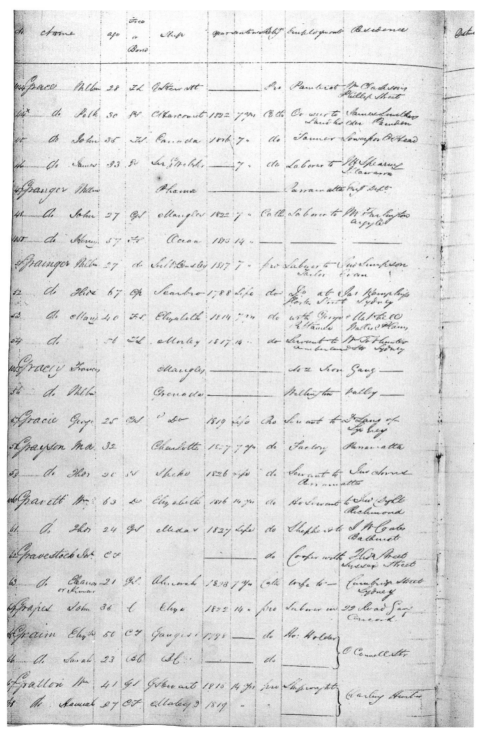

**Figure 26** Census of New South Wales, 1828 (HO 10/23)

Records relating to slave owners in the West Indies, Cape Colony and Mauritius, 1812–1846, are among Treasury, Audit Office and National Debt Office papers (T 71, AO 14, NDO 4). T 71: Office of Registry of Colonial Slaves and Slave Compensation Commission: Records, 1812–1846, consist of registers of the Office for the Registry of Colonial Slaves, 1813 to 1834, most of which are indexed under the names of the owners or plantations; and records of the Slave Compensation Commission, comprising the proceedings of the assistant commissioners who were sent to the several colonies, valuers' returns, registers of claims with indexes, original claims and certificates, counter-claims, adjudications in contested cases, certificates for compensation and lists of awards, commissioners' hearing notes and minutes, accounts, etc.

Among the Chancery Masters' Exhibits, in C 103–C 114, are many private papers from West Indies plantations.

The 1861 England and Wales census was the first for which provision was made for the enumeration of persons on board British ships at sea or in foreign ports; prior to that only ships in territorial waters were covered. Returns from such ships, from 1861 onwards, are found in the special shipping schedules collected together at the end of the census returns. For 1861 only there is a published index to ships' names and an index to names of people on board. This is available at both Kew and the FRC. The FRC only holds a complete set of the decennial census returns for England, Wales, the Channel Islands and Isle of Man, 1841–1891, on microfilm in the following series: HO 107, 1841 and 1851; RG 9, 1861; RG 10, 1871; RG 11, 1881; RG 12, 1891. The returns for 1901, RG 13, are available on-line at both the FRC and Kew. A microfiche set is also available at Kew only.

### 5.2.7 Wills, Probate and Death Duty records

British subjects who died overseas leaving property in England and Wales may have had their wills proved at the Prerogative Court of Canterbury (PCC). The PRO holds PCC wills, 1383–1858, on microfilm, together with administrations, 1559–1858 in the series PROB 11 and PROB 6 respectively. Copies of both are available at the FRC. These series are both indexed in PROB 12 and there are various published name indexes to these series available at both sites. In November 2001 the PCC Wills for the period 1850–58 were put on-line via the PRO web site as part of the PRO's e-business strategy. It is hoped that all records within the PROB 11 series will be available on-line in due course. Wills proved after 1858 are held by the Probate Search Rooms at the Principal Registry of the Family Division, First Avenue House, 42–49 High Holborn, London WC1V 6NP (Tel: 020 7947 6000). However, microfiche copies of the indexes to these wills (The *National Probate Index*), for 1858–1943, can be seen at the PRO and the FRC. The *National Probate Index* provides information about overseas testators and intestates with property in England and Wales, and of course their dates of death and whereabouts. *See also* 2.1.2 for will notices published in Colonial government gazettes. IR 26: Estate Duty Office and predecessors: Registers of Legacy Duty, Succession Duty and Estate Duty, 1796–1903, are also invaluable, providing evidence of deaths of family members abroad as well as those of testate or intestate dying overseas. From 1853, however, English estates of British abroad were exempt from payment of duty. Microfilm copies of IR 26 (to 1857 only) are available at the FRC and at Kew, as are the indexes to them in IR 27. Records after 1857 are stored off-site and need to be requested (in advance) for production at Kew.

## 5.3 Other UK sources

### 5.3.1 Guildhall Library sources

The Bishop of London had a historic jurisdiction over Britons abroad (mostly in Europe). In the nineteenth and early twentieth centuries, the Bishop of London maintained a series of returned registers of miscellaneous baptisms, marriages and burials of British overseas. The volumes are often referred to as the International Memoranda and relate mainly to registers drawn up by chaplains officiating at British embassies abroad. The International Memoranda are available at the Guildhall Library, Manuscripts Section, Aldermanbury, London EC2P 2EJ. The Guildhall Library also holds registers of some Anglican churches overseas and has also published a useful book on this subject: *The British Overseas: A Guide to Records of Their Births, Baptisms, Marriages, Deaths and Burials available in the United Kingdom, Guildhall Library Research Guide 2*, 4th edn, 1994. *The British Overseas* gives full details of sources held by the Guildhall Library, the PRO, the Society of Genealogists and other record offices and libraries throughout the United Kingdom.

### 5.3.2 British Library sources

The Oriental and India Office Collections at the British Library, 96 Euston Road, London NW1 2DP hold a largely complete set of all those colonial registers of births, marriages and deaths for India (1698–1948). These are indexed by Presidency (Bengal, Bombay, Madras). There is also a biographical card index available for consultation in the Oriental and India Office Reading Room. The index is compiled from a variety of sources and contains nearly 300,000 entries for civil and military servants and their families, and for non-official Europeans living in India.

The collection also holds copy registers of births/baptisms, marriages and burials of European and Eurasian Christians in India, Burma and territories controlled from India, together with wills and grants of administration, registered in one of the three Presidencies.

### 5.3.3  Society of Genealogists sources

The Society of Genealogists, 14 Charterhouse Buildings, Goswell Road, London EC1M 7BA holds a number of published and unpublished records relating to life-cycle records of British persons overseas. For example, it holds microfiche copies of, and indexes to, the Australian registers, 1790–1900, of births, marriages and deaths.

### 5.3.4  Lambeth Palace Library sources

The Fulham Papers in the Lambeth Palace Library, London SE1 7JU (Tel: 020 7928 6222), include reports sent to the Bishop of London of eighteenth- and nineteenth-century baptisms, marriages and burials of some of the North American and West Indian colonies, including the Bahamas.

## 5.4  Overseas sources

The British colonies set up their own registers of births, marriages and deaths and these are now usually in the custody of the archives and registry offices of those countries of origin. The addresses of National Archives in overseas countries can usually be found from the latest edition of *The World of Learning* (Europa Publications, London), which is published annually. Many national archives also have Internet sites.

# 6 The British Overseas in Wartime

## 6.1 Prisoners of War

### 6.1.1 Before 1793

There are a number of individual sources concerning British troops captured during the American Revolutionary War and during earlier military and naval actions in North America: consult C M Andrews, *Guide to the Materials for American History to 1783 in the Public Record Office of Great Britain*. A list of names of both British and American officers who were prisoners of war was drawn up in 1781 with a view to an exchange. The list gives the name, rank and corps/regiment of British and German officers who were to be exchanged with American officers of the same rank. It can be found in WO 40/2. Reference to this can also be found among Treasury files in T 64/23 and 24.

The *Calendars of Home Office Papers, George III, 1760–1775*, available in the Map and Large Document Room, include references to some prisoners of war listed in SP 42: State Papers Naval, 1689–1782.

### 6.1.2 The French Wars, 1793–1815

There are lists and accounts of British Prisoners of War (PoWs) in France and elsewhere, which were transmitted by the agent in charge of each prison. The agent recorded, in a numbered sequence, the names, origins and eventual disposal of all the prisoners under his charge. These can be found in ADM 103. They mainly cover naval and civilian prisoners.

### 6.1.3 Crimean War, 1853–1855 and the South African War, 1899–1902

British PoWs captured during the Crimean War, and by the Boers during the South African War, are listed in the *London Gazette* in series ZJ 1. These lists are incomplete, arranged by regiment, and usually list officers only.

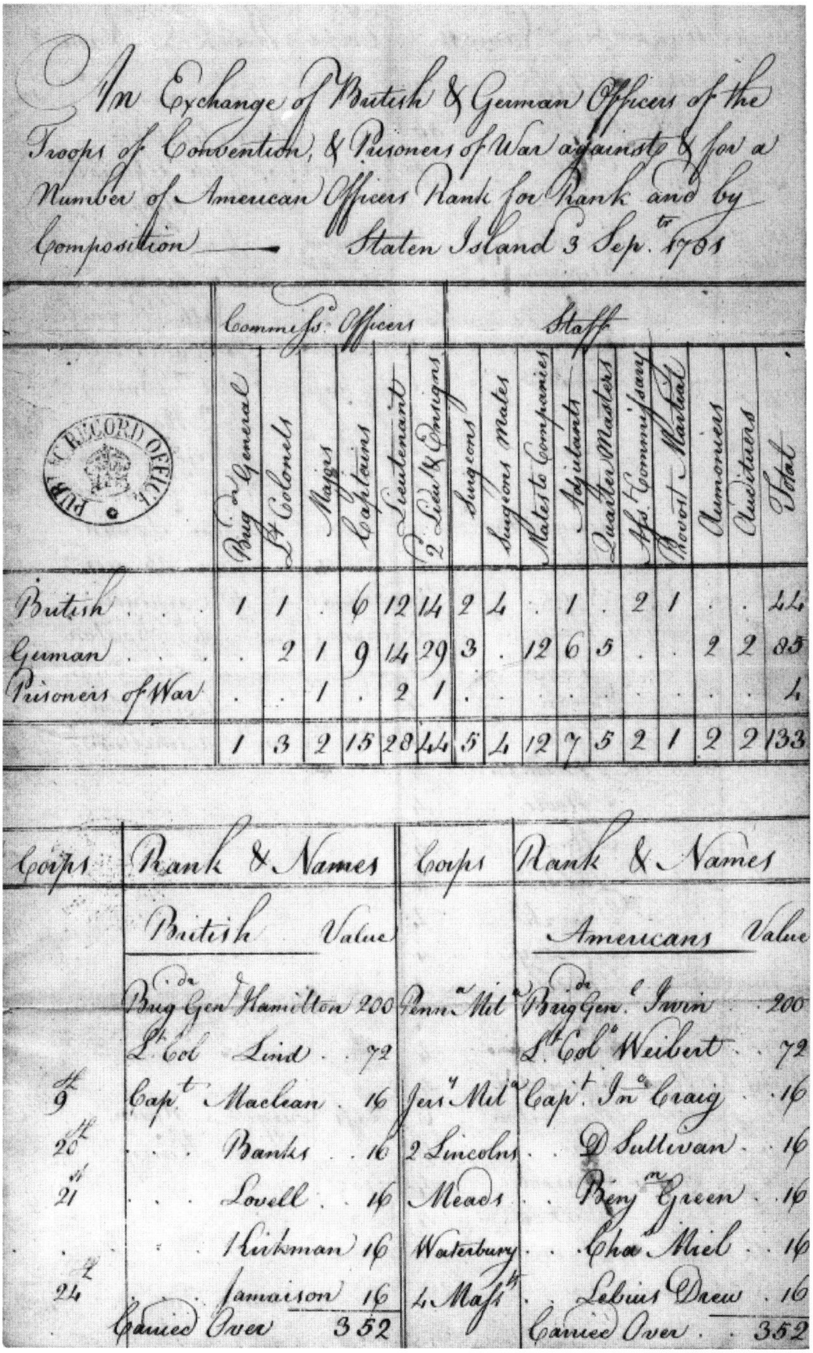

An Exchange of British & German Officers of the Troops of Convention, & Prisoners of War against & for a Number of American Officers Rank for Rank and by Composition — Staten Island 3 Sep.tr 1781

| | Commiss. Officers | | | | | | Staff | | | | | | | | | |
|---|---|---|---|---|---|---|---|---|---|---|---|---|---|---|---|---|
| | Brig.r General | Lt Colonels | Majors | Captains | Lieutenants | 2 Lieuts & Ensigns | Surgeons | Surgeons Mates | Mates to Companies | Adjutants | Quarter Masters | Ass.t Commissary | Provost Marshal | Aumoniers | Auditeurs | Total |
| British | 1 | 1 | . | 6 | 12 | 14 | 2 | 4 | . | 1 | . | 2 | 1 | . | . | 44 |
| German | . | 2 | 1 | 9 | 14 | 29 | 3 | . | 12 | 6 | 5 | . | . | 2 | 2 | 85 |
| Prisoners of War | . | . | 1 | . | 2 | 1 | . | . | . | . | . | . | . | . | . | 4 |
| | 1 | 3 | 2 | 15 | 28 | 44 | 5 | 4 | 12 | 7 | 5 | 2 | 1 | 2 | 2 | 133 |

| Corps | Rank & Names<br>British | Value | Corps | Rank & Names<br>Americans | Value |
|---|---|---|---|---|---|
| | Brig.r Gen.l Hamilton | 200 | Penn.a Mil. | Brig.r Gen.l Irwin | 200 |
| | Lt Col Lind | 72 | | Lt Col.o Weibert | 72 |
| 9th | Capt Maclean | 16 | Jers.y Mil. | Capt. Jn.o Craig | 16 |
| 20th | Banks | 16 | 2 Lincolns | D Sullivan | 16 |
| 21st | Lovell | 16 | Meads | Benj.n Green | 16 |
| . | Kirkman | 16 | Waterbury | Cha. Miel | 16 |
| 24th | Jamaison | 16 | 4 Mass.ts | Lebius Drew | 16 |
| | Carried Over | 352 | | Carried Over | 352 |

**Figure 27** Exchange of Prisoners of War with the United States dated 3 September 1781 (WO 40/2)

## 6.1.4 First World War, 1914–1918

The Public Record Office does not hold a comprehensive list of all British and Commonwealth PoWs. Consequently it can be difficult to establish whether an individual was taken prisoner and, more particularly, if so, in which camp he was interned.

### 6.1.4.1 Officers

The PRO Library holds a publication entitled *List of British Officers taken prisoner in the various Theatres of War between August 1914 and November 1918*. This was compiled by the military agents Cox and Co. in 1919. It is arranged by theatre of war, and then by regiment. It includes an index of regiments at the start of the book, and a name index at the back. The list covers the British Army, Royal Air Force (RAF), the Royal Naval Air Service (RNAS), the Royal Naval Reserve (RNR) and the Royal Naval Division (RND), and gives the name and rank of the officer, the date when he went missing, where and when he was interned (but not the specific camp/s), and the date of his repatriation. If the officer died while a prisoner, the list gives the date and place of death. In addition, officers were required to provide a report concerning the circumstances behind their capture. These, if they survive, may possibly be found in their individual service records in WO 339 and 374.

### 6.1.4.2 Other ranks

There are no known official or published sources to help determine whether an ordinary serviceman or NCO was made a PoW. However, it is possible that this is recorded on their service record or the First World War medal entitlement fiches held in the Microfilm Reading Room. Alternatively, the International Committee of the Red Cross in Geneva keeps an incomplete list of known PoWs and internees of all nationalities for the First World War. Searches are only made in response to written enquiries, and an hourly fee is charged. The address to write to is International Council of the Red Cross, Archives Division, 19 Avenue de la Paix, CH-1202, Geneva.

### 6.1.4.3 Searching for an individual

Ask at the Research Enquiries Desk for the guide *Researching British and Commonwealth Prisoners of War: World War One*. This indicates which PRO sources are most likely to provide personal details and includes: copies of nominal indexes of British, Irish, Colonial and Indian PoWs extracted from WO 161/101; references to nominal lists of Military and Merchant Navy PoWs; a list of PoW camps in Germany and enemy territory; an indexed map of the main PoW camps in Germany and Austria.

The primary source for personal information are the reports made by Officers, Medical Officers, Other Ranks, and occasionally Merchant Seamen and Civilians, held in WO 161/95–100 and indexed by WO 161/101. As well as narrative, these reports can include details of unit, home address, when and where captured, wounds suffered, transfer between camps, comments on treatment and conditions and escape attempts.

Both Military and Merchant Navy PoWs can also be searched for by name within the card index to Foreign Office correspondence located in the Research Enquiries Room. If an entry is found this will usually lead to an FO 383 reference, although it must be stressed that only a small percentage of these records has survived. Other Merchant Navy PoW records are contained in MT 9 (code 106), which includes some files indexed by individual name and/or ship. In addition, for Royal Navy, Royal Naval Air Service, Royal Naval Reserve and Royal Naval Volunteer Reserve PoWs try searching the ADM 12 registers, although, because of the complex nature of these records, this can be time consuming with no guarantee of success. For the RAF, Royal Flying Corps and Royal Naval Air Service try the Air Historical Branch (AHB) indexes located among the additional finding aids in the Research Enquiries Room.

### 6.1.4.4  Deaths of Prisoners of War 1914–1918

Deaths of PoWs and internees occurring in military and non-military hospitals, and in enemy and occupied territory, were notified to British authorities by foreign embassies, legations, registration authorities and American authorities in charge of British internees. The record series RG 35/45–69 (Microfilm Reading Room, Kew, and at the Family Records Centre) contains an incomplete collection of these certificates, which are largely written in French. In addition, PoWs who died while captive are recorded in registers held in the Family Records Centre; *see* 5.1.1.

### 6.1.4.5  Other sources

Records concerning PoW camps and related subjects are mostly found in two record series. The most comprehensive are the reports held in WO 161/95–100, which can be accessed by using the place and subject indexes in WO 161/101. Individual camps can also be searched for by name in the card index to Foreign Office correspondence, held in the Research Enquiries Room, Kew. This contains references to the files of the Prisoners of War and Aliens Department (FO 383:1915–1919) set up to deal with all matters relating to conditions for prisoners, repatriation and general policy. Each year within the index has a dedicated PoW section arranged by country and subject. Further records relating to PoW camps, administration and policy are found in CO 693, with related registers in CO 754 and CO 755. Records of the Committee on the Treatment by the Enemy of British PoWs (1914–1919) are in HO 45/10763/270829, and HO 45/10764/270829, with additional material in WO 162.

## 6.1.5 Second World War, 1939–1945

### 6.1.5.1 All services

The International Committee of the Red Cross in Geneva keeps an incomplete list of known PoWs and internees of all nationalities for the Second World War. Searches are only made in response to written enquiries, and an hourly fee is charged. The address to write to is International Council of the Red Cross, Archives Division, 19 Avenue de la Paix, CH-1202, Geneva.

There are no central UK lists of British servicemen who were prisoners of war. However, the PRO Library holds alphabetical registers of British and Dominion POWs of all ranks who were held in Germany and German occupied territories. They give details of name, rank and service/army number as well as regiment/corps, prisoner of war number and camp location details. The lists are correct generally up to 30 March 1945, and are in three volumes: British Army; Armies and other Land Forces of the British Empire; Naval and Air Forces of Great Britain and the Empire.

Also at the PRO in the Research Enquiries Room, ask for the folder 'British Prisoners of War: World War Two'. This provides full document references, dates and descriptions, for: Reports on Prisoner of War Camps; Prisoner of War Lists; Prisoner of War escape and evasion reports; Miscellaneous reports.

### 6.1.5.2 War Office records

WO 347: Allied Prisoners of War Hospitals, Thailand and Burma, Registers and Papers, Second World War, 1942–1947 consist of admission and discharge registers, alphabetical sick registers and death registers, kept by prisoners of war at Nong Pladock Camp and its Ubon or Oubone satellite, in Thailand. There is also an official war diary and death register of the disease-ravaged Tanbaya Hospital Camp in Burma, including an account of the move from Singapore to Thailand, and a War Office PoW Casualty Section file relating to the registers. The contents of each of these registers are diverse and complicated in arrangement, which has necessitated detailed collation in each. To assist researchers, details of the collation are filed at the front of each piece.

The War Office Registered Files (WO 32 code 91) and the Directorate of Military Operations Collation Files (WO 193/343–359) both contain material on Allied POWs. The Military Headquarters Papers: SHAEF (GI Division) contain files relating to the organization of the Prisoners of War Executive and reports on Allied PoWs (WO 219/1402, 1448–1474). Some of these documents are subject to extended closure. The War Diary of MI9, the division of Military Intelligence which dealt with escaped prisoners of all services and those who evaded capture, is in WO 165/39, and its papers are in WO 208/3242–3566. These include camp histories (some with aerial photographs), escape and liberation reports, and files on MI9 staff, some of which are subject to extended closure. The nominal card indexes to the three main series of escape, evasion and liberation reports in WO 208 are available in the Research Enquiries Room. For the uninitiated, these were made by all ranks of the British and Commonwealth armed forces and merchant navy, and occasionally American service personnel. However, it should be noted that they mostly relate to those serving in the European/Mediterranean theatres of war and only represent a small percentage of the estimated 192,000 British and Commonwealth PoWs.

They are an invaluable source of personal information and usually include: service details; when and where captured; home address and civilian occupation; and, for RAF personnel, details of where based, type of aircraft, when, where and how the aircraft was lost, and the presumed fate of the other aircrew. Every report has a narrative, of variable length, which describes an individual's experiences as an escaper, evader and/or prisoner of war.

In addition, many reports include appendices. These are indicated on the card by an X against the appropriate lettercode/s from A–D; nevertheless, it is unlikely all appendices have survived. Furthermore, some cards include references to other reports in the same series or a different series, while others have references which are obsolete, whose meaning and purpose is unknown, or which may refer to unreleased or destroyed documents.

Medical reports on conditions in PoW camps, with some reports on escapes, are among the Medical Historian's Papers in WO 222/1352–1393. Details of war crimes committed against Allied PoWs have been preserved among the Judge Advocate General's War Crimes Papers, in WO 235.

The minutes of the Imperial Prisoners of War Committee, 1941–1945, are in WO 163/582–593.

### 6.1.5.3 Air Ministry records

Records concerning RAF and Allied Air Force prisoners will be found in the correspondence of the Air Ministry in AIR 2 code B 89, as well as in the Unregistered Papers (PoWs) in AIR 20 code 89. Nominal rolls for individual camps, principally Japanese, are among papers prepared for a history of the RAF medical services, in AIR 49/383–388. An alphabetical list of British and Dominion Air Force PoWs in German hands in 1944–1945 is in AIR 20/2336. Nominal rolls of prisoners in Stalag Luft III and Stalag IIIA are in AIR 40/1488–91.

A substantial quantity of material concerning British and Dominion PoWs, mostly Air

Force personnel, can be found in the Headquarters Papers of Bomber Command (AIR 14) and in the Air Ministry's Directorate of Intelligence Papers (AIR 40). Location lists and some aerial photographs of PoW camps in Germany, Italy and occupied Europe, including reports on transfers, are in AIR 14/1235–1240, and similar documentation on German camps occurs in AIR 40/227–231. Reports of escaped RAF personnel, including some nominal lists of reported Air Force PoWs, are in AIR 14/353–361; these files deal mainly with aids to escape and conduct in enemy territory. Similar material, with reports on German interrogation methods, is in AIR 14/461–465. Reports of RAF and Dominion Air Force escapers, including lists of PoWs in enemy hands, can also be found in AIR 40/1545–1552. Reports on many individual RAF servicemen taken prisoner in occupied Europe, detailing the circumstances of their capture, are in AIR 14/470 and 471. Reports on the condition of British and Dominion PoWs in German and Japanese camps towards the end of the war occur in AIR 40/2361 and 2366.

### 6.1.5.4 Admiralty and Board of Trade records

A list of all Royal Marines known to have been held in German camps between 1939 and 1945 is to be found in ADM 201/111.

The Prisoners of War and Internment Files in the Admiralty and Secretariat Papers (ADM 1 code 79) contain documentation on many aspects of the Royal Navy's involvement with the capture and internment of enemy and Allied PoWs, naval and other services.

BT 373: Board of Trade: Registrar General of Shipping and Seamen: Merchant Seamen Prisoner of War Records; War of 1939–1945 consist of pouches recording the circumstances of capture and the eventual fate of merchant seamen captured during the war of 1939–1945. BT 373/1 to BT 373/359 are indexed by ship's name which was captured or lost due to enemy action. These contain miscellaneous papers relating to the circumstances of loss/capture.

BT 373/360 to BT 373/3716 contain individual pouches of seamen respectively. Each pouch typically contains the following papers/details: name of the ship lost usually written in red ink on the PoW envelope; a card or form containing circumstantial details (including PoW camp, PoW number, surname, christian names, date of birth, place of birth, discharge A number, rank or rating, name of ship, ship's official number, date of loss of ship, next of kin, relationship, address and country of detention); Prisoner of War Branch PC 96 (postal censorship) forms vetting messages to and from family and friends; Envelope RS3 which usually has notes of release from captivity/repatriation written on it where appropriate, containing many of the details from the PoW card and additionally a National Service AF Account Number. Some of the pouches may also contain personal letters to and from prisoners of war. Collective alphabetical listings of prisoners of war (as opposed to individual pouches) are contained in BT 373/3717 and in BT 373/3720 to BT 373/3722. BT 373/3720 and BT 373/3721 consist of lists of prisoners of war who died in captivity in Japan and Germany.

### 6.1.5.5 Foreign Office and Colonial Office sources

Diplomatic correspondence with the Red Cross and the Protecting Powers is in the files of the Foreign Office Consular (War) Department in FO 916, and the reports of these organizations on enemy PoW camps and hospitals are in WO 224. Colonial Office files on British prisoners and internees in the Far East, and British Colonial prisoners in Europe, occur in CO 980: Prisoners of War and Civilian Internees Department, 1941–1953, and CO 537: Confidential General and Confidential Original Correspondence. Of particular interest are CO 980/131: Red Cross lists of British Colonial prisoners of war and civilian internees in Germany and Italy, 1943–1944; CO 537/1220: Malaya: Conditions in Changi Camp, 1943–1946; and CO 537/1221: Camps in the Far East: Malaya.

The *Index to General Correspondence* of the Foreign Office, 1920–1951 (available at the PRO) contains numerous entries relating to PoWs, displaced persons and refugees. The bulk of the correspondence that has been preserved is in FO 371.

### 6.1.5.6 Other sources

Papers dealing with the treatment of British PoWs in German hands are in DEFE 2/1126, DEFE 2/1127, DEFE 2/1128. Policy discussions concerning Allied PoWs are in CAB 122. Correspondence on British merchant seamen taken prisoner occurs in MT 9 code 106.

## 6.2 Internment

During the First and Second World Wars British civilians resident in enemy occupied territory were interned. In both wars, internment camps were established within such areas and the PRO holds records relating to this subject among the archives of the Home Office (HO), Colonial Office (CO) and Foreign Office (FO).

### 6.2.1 First World War

Very few records of individual internees survive for the First World War. References to individual internees can be found in the card index to the Foreign Office general correspondence in the Research Enquiries Room. Any reference found on a card needs to be coverted into a modern PRO reference: for guidance on doing this, *see* 'Overseas Records Information' leaflet 12.

### 6.2.2 Second World War: policy

A Consular (War) Department, soon renamed the Prisoners of War Department, was established in the Foreign Office in January 1942 to handle matters relating to British subjects who became classed as enemy aliens and prisoners of war in enemy and enemy occupied countries.

### 6.2.3 Second World War: personal records

References to individual internees and internment camps may be found in the printed indexes of the general correspondence of the Foreign Office, available in the Research Enquiries Room.

Other Foreign Office records relating to British citizens resident overseas and interned by the enemy forces are in FO 916: Consular (War) Department, later Prisoners of War Department: Registered Files (KW and RD Series), 1939–1948. This series contains registered files of the Consular (War) Department, later the Prisoners of War Department and comprises reports from various sources on prisoners of war and internment camps in enemy and enemy occupied countries and on the treatment of British subjects both military and civilian. Other matters dealt with include welfare, exchange, repatriations, escapes and deaths. Various lists of British subjects interned in camps also survive among this series. These relate mainly to camps located in the Far East, namely, the Phillipines, Hong Kong, Japan, Manchuria, Siam, China and the Dutch East Indies.

Later reports are in WO 224: War Office: International Red Cross and Protecting Powers (Geneva): Reports concerning Prisoner of War Camps in Europe and the Far East, 1941–1947. This series consists primarily of a collection of reports by the International Red Cross and Protecting Powers (Geneva) and deals with conditions and events in various prisoner of war camps in Europe and the Far East.

Information about enemy aliens and internees in the colonies can be found in CO 968: Defence: Original Correspondence, 1941–1965 and CO 980: Prisoners of War and Civilian Internees Department, 1941–1953.

CO 968 contains records of the Defence Departments, comprising files dealing with all aspects of the defence and security of the colonial empire including matters of policy and internal security. CO 980 contains files of the Prisoners of War, Civilian Internees and Casualties Department. A large part of this collection of papers concerns civilian internees detained when Singapore and Hong Kong were invaded by Japan. There are also files on the conditions in internee camps. Notable documents within this series

BRITISCHE STAATSANGEHOERIGE, DIE IN BIBERACH, WUERTTEMBERG,
( OFLAG 55 VD) INTERNIERT WURDEN, laut Mitteilung des O.K.W.
No. 11 vom 2. Oktober 1942.

| No. | Name | Geburtsort und -tag | naechster Verwandter | Beruf | letzter Wohnort | Tag der Festnahme |
|-----|------|---------------------|----------------------|-------|-----------------|-------------------|
| 1 | ABERNETHY Staniel | 11.November 1901 London | Wiverton Road 99, London SE 21 | Agent | Tehocy Channel isles | Jersey 18/9/42 |
| 2 | ABERNETHY Daisy | 9. Jan. 1896 London | Winifred Elliott Howell's Scholl Liandaff, Cardiff, Sout Wales | Hausfrau | Jersey | Jersey |
| 3 | ADAMS Arthur | 28. Mai 1880 Wolver-Hampton | C.Adams Villiers Avenue Bilston, Staffordshire | - - - | Bel Royal Jersey | 16/9/ 194 |
| 4 | ADAMS Marie | 1. Aug. 1881 London | Rebel, 40 Avenue Paris | Hausfrau | Jersey | " " |
| 5 | ALDOUS Thomas | 5. Jan. 1888 Libton | 1,Don Road, St. Helier, Jersey | Arbeiter | " | " " |
| 6 | AGER Jack | 3. Maerz 1897 Fordhain | Mill Lane,Fordham, Cambs. | Kellner | " | " |
| 7 | Amoore Gordon | 26. Maerz 1878 Bornmouth | E.Amoore,St.Helens R.D.,Hastings | Zahnarzt | " | " |
| 8 | ANDERSON Stanley | 12. Juli 1916 London | T.Anderson,35 Treaford Lane,Wardend | Autome- chaniker | " | " |
| 9 | ANDREWS Jeremiah | 30.Juni 1905 Danhington | J.Andrews,Birming- ham,Darlington | Holzhaendler" | " | " |
| 10 | ANDREWES Zeonest | 24. Dez.1881 London | 22 Chaldon Way, Coulsdon,Surey | Gemuese- haendler | " | " |
| 11 | ARBUCKLE Huch | 12. Aug.1871 Yorkshire | ARBUCKLE,Quentin 14,RoyalStone Road | - - - | " | " |
| 12 | ARBUCKLE Julie | 4. Juni 1884 Palhousie,India | 14 Royston Road Bradford | Hausfrau | " | " 18/9/42 |
| 13 | ARMSTRONG Rosina | 10.Sept.1910 Bath,Somerset | Laycock Kotton, Wiltshire, Mrs.P.Brunt | Hausdame | " | " |
| 14 | ASHDOWN Leonard | 20.Juli 1888 London | Mrs.Smith,23 Sher- wood Rd.Greenford Middelsex | Verkaeufer | " | " 16/9/42 |
| 15 | ASHDOWN Florence | 25.Mai 1892 York | Miss Myers,41 Kirby Rd.Portsmouth | - - - | Mount Wisey Plamorah,Jersey | " |
| 16 | ASTE Percy | 9. Sept.1873 Norwood | 15 Midvale Road Jersey | - - - | Jersey,4 Hill- crest Aven- | 18/9/42 |
| 17 | ASTE Evelyn | 5. Dez. 1882 Jersey | " | - - - | " | " 19/9/42 |

**Figure 28** Evacuation of Channel Islands and German occupation: lists of people deported to Germany (HO 144/22920 (pt 2))

include CO 980/119: Lists of civilian internees in camps in the Far East, 1942–1946; CO 980/131: Red Cross lists of British Colonial prisoners of war and civilian internees in Germany and Italy, 1943–1944; CO 980/203: Nominal roll of Colonial merchant seamen interned in Germany and Japan, 1944; CO 980/208: Official Japanese lists of British civilians who died in internment camps in Malaya, 1943–1946; and CO 980/230: Nominal roll of civilian internees released from Stanley camp, Hong Kong, 1945. There is a separate series of registers of correspondence to this series in CO 1012. Some records within CO 980 are closed for 75 years.

On the 7 November 2000, the British Government announced a single ex gratia payment of £10,000 to be paid to the surviving members of the British groups who were held prisoner by the Japanese during the Second World War. The scheme is administered by the War Pensions Agency (WPA) and you can contact the War Pensions Agency on Freeline 0800 169 22 77 for more information and to request a claim form. At the time of writing this Guide, many of the above series of records have been requested back by the War Pensions Agency to enable them to seek additional information in order to confirm entitlement. The WPA can also be contacted in writing at the War Pensions Agency, Norcross, Blackpool FY5 3WP or via e-mail at warpensions@gtnet.gov.uk. Their web site address is www.dss.gov.uk/wpa/index.htm.

For those interested in tracing records of British personnel interned in the Channel Islands following the German invasion in 1940, the following document may be of use: HO 144/22920: Channel Islands: Evacuation of Channel Islands and German occupation: lists of people deported to Germany.

# Bibliography

## General

L Atherton, *'Never Complain, Never Explain': Records of the Foreign Office and State Paper Office, 1500–c.1960* (Public Record Office, 1994)

P Bean and J Melville, *Lost Children of the Empire* (Unwin Hyman Ltd, London, 1989)

*Calendars of Home Office Papers, George III, 1760–1775*

*Calendar of State Papers, Colonial, America and West Indies, 1574–1738* (London, 1860–1969)

*Calendar of State Papers East Indies, 1513–1668*, 5 vols

*Calendar of Treasury Books, 1660–1718* (London, 1904–62)

*Calendar of Treasury Papers, 1557–1728* (London, 1868–89)

*Calendar of Treasury Books and Papers, 1729–1745* (London, 1898–1903)

W A Carrothers, *Emigration from the British Isles* (Frank Cass and Co., London, 1965)

C Erickson, *Emigration from Europe 1815–1914* (Adam and Charles Black, London, 1976)

General Register Office, *Abstract of Arrangements Respecting Registration of Births, Marriages and Deaths in the United Kingdom and the Other Countries of the British Commonwealth of Nations, and in the Irish Republic* (London, 1952)

J S W Gibson, 'Assisted Pauper Emigration, 1834–1837', *Genealogists' Magazine* XX, pp. 374–5

A James Hammerton, *Emigrant Gentlewomen* (Croom Helm, London, 1979)

*Journals of the Board of Trade and Plantations, 1704–1782* (London, 1920–38)

R B Pugh, *The Records of the Colonial and Dominions Office* (Public Record Office, London, 1964)

Public Record Office, *Alphabetical Guide to Certain War Office and Other Military Records*

Public Record Office, *The Records of the Foreign Office 1782–1939* (London, 1969)

Public Record Office *Records preserved in the Public Record Office, Lists and Indexes*, vol. LIII (London, 1931)

Public Record Office, *List of Colonial Office Records*, Lists and Indexes, vol. XXXVI (London, 1911)

Public Record Office, *List of Records of the Treasury, Paymaster General's Office, Exchequer and Audit Department and Board of Trade, prior to 1837*, Lists and Indexes vol. XLVI (London, 1922)

Public Record Office, *List of State Papers, Domestic, 1547–1792, and Home Office Records, 1782–1837, Lists and Indexes*, vol. XLIII (London, 1914)

R B Pugh, *The Records of the Colonial and Dominions Office* (HMSO, London, 1964)

K Smith, C T Watts and M J Watts, *Records of Merchant Shipping and Seamen* (Public Record Office, 1998)

A Thurston, *Records of the Colonial Office, Dominions Office, Commonwealth Relations Office and Commonwealth Office* (HMSO, London, 1995)

G Yeo, *The British Overseas: A Guide to Records of Their Births, Baptisms, Marriages, Deaths and Burials Available in the United Kingdom*, 4th edn (Guildhall Library, London, 1994)


### North America and West Indies

'AMDG', 'Ships, Merchants and Passengers to the American Colonies 1618–1688' (unpublished MS, dated Purley 1982). [Taken from the Port Books in E 190.]

C M Andrews, *Guide to the Materials for American History to 1783 in the Public Record Office of Great Britain* (Carnegie Institute of Washington, Washington, 1912 and 1914)

C E Banks and E E Brownell, *Topographical Dictionary of 2885 English Emigrants to New England, 1620–1650* (Southern Book Company, Baltimore, 1957)

C Boyer (ed.), *Ships' Passenger Lists: The South* (1538–1825); *National and New England* (1600–1825); *New York and New Jersey* (1600–1825); *Pennsylvania and Delaware* (1641–1825) (4 vols, Newhall, California, 1980)

M Bradner, *The Emigrant Scots: Why they left and where they went* (Constable, London, 1982)

J M Brock, *The Mobile Scot: A Study of Emigration and Migration 1861* (John Donald Publishers, Edinburgh, 1999)

M J Burchall, 'Parish-Organised Emigration to America', *Genealogists' Magazine* XVIII, pp. 336–42

W Cameron and M McDougall Maude, *Assisting Emigration to Upper Canada: The Petworth Project 1832–1837* (McGill-Queens University Press, Montreal, 2000)

W Cameron, S Haines and M McDougall Maude, *English Emigrant Voices: Labourers' Letters from Upper Canada in the 1830s* (McGill-Queens University Press, Montreal, 2000)

P W Coldham, *American Loyalist Claims* (National Genealogical Society, Washington, 1980) (Indexes AO 13/1–35, 37, which contain claims for compensation from American loyalists who escaped to Canada, 1774–93.)

P W Coldham, *American Migration* (Genealogical Publishing Company, Baltimore, 2000)

P W Coldham, *Bonded Passengers to America, 1615–1775* (Genealogical Publishing Company, Baltimore, 1983)

P W Coldham, *The Bristol Registers of Servants Sent to Foreign Plantations 1654–1686* (Genealogical Publishing Company, Baltimore, 1988)

P W Coldham, *The Complete Book of Emigrants, 1607–1776* (4 vols, Genealogical Publishing Company, Baltimore, 1987–93)

P W Coldham, *Emigrants from England to the American Colonies, 1773–1776* (Genealogical Publishing Company, Baltimore, 1988)

P W Coldham, *English Adventurers and Emigrants, 1609–1660 Abstracts of Examinations in the High Court of Admiralty, with Reference to Colonial America* (Genealogical Publishing Company, Baltimore, 1984)

P W Coldham, *English Estates of American Colonists: American Wills and Administrations in the Prerogative Court of Canterbury, 1610–1699 and 1700–1799* (Genealogical Publishing Company, Baltimore, 1980)

P W Coldham, *English Estates of American Settlers: American Wills and Administrations in the Prerogative Court of Canterbury, 1800–1858* (Genealogical Publishing Company, Baltimore, 1981)

P W Coldham, *King's Passengers: Transportation coming into Maryland, Virginia* (Family Lines Publications, Westminster, Maryland, 1998–9)

P W Coldham, *Lord Mayor's Court of London, Depositions relating to America, 1641–1736* (National Genealogical Society, Washington, 1980)

P W Coldham. *The King's Passengers to Maryland and Virginia* (Family Line Publications, Westminster, Maryland, 1997)

P W Coldham, *American Migrations 1765–1799* (Genealogical Publishing Company, Baltimore, 2000)

T Coleman, *Passage to America* (Hutchinson, London, 1972)

D Cressy, *Coming Over: Migration and Communication between England and New England in the Seventeenth Century* (Cambridge University Press, Cambridge, 1987)

N K Crowder, *British Army Pensioners Abroad, 1772–1899* (Genealogical Publishing Company, Baltimore, 1995)

N Currer-Briggs, 'American Colonial Gleanings from Town Depositions', *Genealogists' Magazine* XVIII, pp. 288–94

L M DeGrazia and D F Haberstroh, *Irish Relatives and Friends from 'Information Wanted' Ads in the Irish-American, 1850–1871* (Genealogical Publishing Company, Baltimore, 2001)

D Dobson, *The Original Scots Colonists of Early America 1612–1783* (Genealogical Publishing Company, Baltimore, 1989)

D Dobson, *Scottish Emigration to Colonial America 1607–1785* (University of Georgia Press, Georgia, 1994)

A Douglas, 'Genealogical Research in Canada', *Genealogists' Magazine* XXIII, pp. 217–21

A Douglas, 'Gentlemen Adventurers and Remittance Men' [Hudson's Bay Company], *Genealogists' Magazine* XXIV, pp. 55–9

A R Ekirch, *Bound for America: The Transportation of British Convicts to the Colonies, 1718–1775* (Clarendon Press, Oxford, 1990)

R H Ellis, 'Records of the American Loyalists' Claims in the Public Record Office', *Genealogists' Magazine* XII, pp. 375–8, 407–10, 433–5

C Erickson, *Invisible Immigrants: The Adaptation of English and Scottish Immigrants in 19th-century America* (Cornell University Press, Ithaca, New York, 1972)

C Erickson, *Essays on British Emigration in the Nineteenth Century* (Cornell University Press, Ithaca, New York 1994)

P W Filby, *American and British Genealogy and Heraldry*, 2nd edn (American Library Association, Chicago, 1975)

P W Filby (ed.), *Passenger and Immigration Lists Bibliography 1538–1900* (Gale Research Company, Detroit, 1981)

P W Filby and M K Meyer (ed.), *Passenger and Immigration Lists Index*, 13 vols (Gale Research Company, Detroit, 1981–1995). (Lists approximately 2,410,000 names of immigrants to USA and Canada, from the sixteenth to mid-twentieth centuries)

D H Fischer, *Albion's Seed: Four British Folkways in America* (Oxford University Press, Oxford, 1989)

W Foot, ''That most precious Jewel' – East Florida 1763–83', *Genealogists' Magazine* XXIV, pp. 144–8

A Games, *Migration and the Origins of the English Atlantic World* (Harvard University Press, Cambridge, Massachusetts, 1999)

M S Giuseppi, 'Naturalizations of Foreign Protestants in the American and West Indian colonies', *Huguenot Society* XXIV, 1921

I A Glazier and M Tepper, *The Famine Immigrants: Lists of Irish Immigrants Arriving at the Port of New York, 1846–1851* (Genealogical Publishing Company, Baltimore, 1983)

G Grannum, *Tracing Your West Indian Ancestors* (Public Record Office, 1995)

A C Hollis Hallett, *Early Bermuda Records 1619–1826* (Juniper Hill Press, Bermuda, 1991)

J C Hotten, *Original Lists of Persons Emigrating to America, 1600–1700* (London, 1874)

J Hunter, *A Dance Called America: The Scottish Highlands, the United States and Canada* (Mainstream Publishing, Edinburgh, 1994)

C B Jewson, 'Transcript of Three Registers of Passengers from Great Yarmouth to Holland and New England, 1637–1639', *Norfolk Record Society* XXV (1954)

J Kaminkow and M Kaminkow, *A list of Emigrants from England to America, 1718–1759* (Magna Carta Book Company, Baltimore, 1964)

J Kaminkow and M Kaminkow, *Original Lists of Emigrants in Bondage from London to the American Colonies 1719–1744* (Magna Carta Book Company, Baltimore, 1981)

S C Johnson, *Emigration from the United Kingdom to North America 1763–1912* (Frank Cass and Company, London, 1966)

*Journals of the Board of Trade and Plantations, 1704–1782* (London, 1920–1938)

W A Knittle, *Early Eighteenth Century Palatine Emigration* (Dorrance and Company, Philadelphia, 1937)

A H Lancour, *A Bibliography of Ships' Passenger Lists, 1538–1825* (New York Public Library, New York, 1963)

E Laxton, *The Famine Ships: The Irish Exodus to America* (Henry Holt and Company, New York, 1996)

G E McCracken, 'State and Federal Sources for American Genealogy', *Genealogists' Magazine* XIX, pp. 138–40

M E MacSorley, *Genealogical sources in the United States of America* (self-published, Basingstoke, 1995)

L D MacWethy, *The Book of Names especially relating to the Early Palatines and the First Settlers in the Mohawk Valley* (Genealogical Publishing Company, New York, 1981)

B Merriman, 'Genealogy in Canada', *Genealogists' Magazine* XIX, pp. 306–11

National Archives and Record Service, *A Guide to Genealogical Research in the National Archives* (Washington, 1982)

*New York Genealogical and Biographical Records*, vols XL and LXI (New York, 1909 and 1910) (for Palatine emigrants)

J P Reid and S Fowler, *Genealogical Research in England's Public Record Office: A Guide for North Americans*, 2nd edn (Genealogical Publishing Company, Baltimore, 2000)

W S Shepperson, *British Emigration to North America* (University of Minnesota Press, Minneapolis, 1957)

G Sherwood, *American Colonists in English Records* (2 vols, London, 1932, 1933). (Lists passengers not mentioned in Hotten)

W S Shepperton, *British Emigration to North America* (Blackwell, Oxford, 1957)

C J Stanford, 'Genealogical Sources in Barbados', *Genealogists' Magazine* XVII, pp. 489–98

M Tepper (ed.), *New World Immigrants*, (Genealogical Publishing Company, Baltimore, 1980) (a consolidation of passenger lists)

M Tepper, *Passengers to America: A Consolidation of Ship Passenger Lists from the New England Genealogical Register* (Genealogical Publishing Company, Baltimore, 1988)

M Tepper, *American Passengers Arrival Records* (Baltimore, 1993)

E Thompson (ed.), *The Emigrants' Guide to North America* (Natural Heritage Books, Toronto, 1998)

W E Van Vugt, *Britain to America: Mid-Nineteenth Century Immigrants to the United States* (University of Illinois Press, Chicago, 1999)

D Whyte, *A Dictionary of Scottish Emigrants to the USA* (Genealogical Publishing Company, Baltimore, 1972)

D Whyte, *A Dictionary of Scottish Emigrants to Canada, Volumes I and II* (Ontario Genealogical Society, 1985 and 1995)

### Australia and New Zealand

C Bateson, *The Convict Ships, 1787–1868,* 2nd edn (Brown, Son and Ferguson, Glasgow, 1969)

C J Baxter, *Musters and Lists New South Wales and Norfolk Island, 1800–1802* (ABGR in association with the Australasian Society of Genealogists, Sydney, 1988)

C J Baxter, *Musters New South Wales, Norfolk Island and Van Diemen's Land, 1811* (ABGR in association with the Australasian Society of Genealogists, Sydney, 1987)

C J Baxter, *General Muster and Land and Stock Muster of New South Wales, 1822* (ABGR Sydney, 1988)

A Bromell, *Tracing Family History in New Zealand* (Wellington, 1997)

P Burns and H Richardson, *Fatal Success: A History of the New Zealand Company* (Heinemann Reed, Auckland, 1989)

N G Butlin, C W Cromwell and K L Suthern, *General Return of convicts in NSW 1837* (ABGR in association with the Australasian Society of Genealogists, Sydney, 1987)

P G Fidlon and R J Ryan (eds), *The First Fleeters* (Australian Documents Library, Sydney, 1981)

Y Fitzmaurice, *Army Deserters from HM Service* (Forest Hill, Victoria, 1988, continuing)

M Flynn, *The Second Fleet: Britain's grim convict armada of 1790* (Library of Australian History Sydney, 1993)

G Fothergill, *A List of Emigrant Ministers to Australia 1690–1811* (London, 1904)

Friends of the East Sussex Record Office, *East Sussex Sentences of Transportation at Quarter Sessions, 1790–1854* (Lewes, 1988)

M Gillen, *The Founders of Australia, A Biographical Dictionary of the First Fleet* (Library of Australian History, Sydney, 1989)

D T Hawkings, *Bound for Australia* (Phillimore, Guildford, 1987)

H Hughes and L Hughes, *Discharged in New Zealand – Soldiers of the Imperial Foot Regiments who took their discharge in New Zealand 1840–1870* (Auckland, 1988)

R Hughes, *The Fatal Shore: A History of Transportation of Convicts to Australia, 1781–1868* (Collins Harvill, London, 1987)

L Marshall and V Mossong, 'Genealogical Research in New Zealand', *Genealogists' Magazine* XX, pp. 45–9

J Melton, *Ship's Deserters 1852–1900* (Library of Australian History, Sydney, 1986)

A G Peake, *Bibliography of Australian Family History* (Dulwich, South Australia, 1988)

A G Peake, *National Register of Shipping Arrivals: Australia and New Zealand* (Australasia Federation of Family History Organisations Inc., Sydney, 1992)

L L Robson, *The Convict Settlers of Australia* (Melbourne University Press, Melbourne, 1981)

R J Ryan, *The Second Fleet Convicts* (Australian Documents Library, Sydney, 1982)

M R Sainty and K A Johnson (eds), *New South Wales: Census, November 1828* (Library of Australian History, Sydney, 1980)

E Stokes, *Innocents Abroad. The Story of Child Evacuees in Australia 1940–45* (Allan and Unwin, London, 1994)

N Vine Hall, *Tracing your Family History in Australia – A Guide to Sources* (London, 1985)

H Woolcock, *Rights of Passage: Emigration to Australia in the 19th Century* (Tavistock, London, 1986)

I Wyatt (ed.), *Transportees from Gloucester to Australia, 1783–1842* (Bristol and Gloucester Archaeological Society, 1988)

## South Africa

E Bull, *Aided Immigration to South Africa, 1857–1867* (Human Sciences Research Council, Pretoria, 1991)

R J Lombard, 'Genealogical Research in South Africa', *Genealogists' Magazine* (Society of Genealogists, London), XIX, pp. 274–6

E Morse Jones, *Rolls of the British Settlers in South Africa* (Cape Town, 1971)

P Philip, *British Residents at the Cape 1795–1819* (Cape Town, 1981)

## South East Asia

I A Baxter, *Brief Guide to Biographical Sources in the India Office Library* (The British Library, London, 1979)

British Library, *India Office Records, Sources for Family History Research* (The British Library, London, 1988)

*East India Register* (various titles)

I V Fitzhugh, 'East India Company Ancestry', *Genealogists' Magazine* (Society of Genealogists, London) XXI, pp. 150–54

*India [Office and Burma Office] List, 1791–1947*

*Indian Army List, 1901–1939*

M Moir, *A General Guide to the India Office Records* (The British Library, London, 1988)

Society of Genealogists, *Sources for Anglo-Indian Genealogy in the Library of the Society of Genealogists* (1990)

J Wall, 'The British Association for Cemeteries in South Asia', *Genealogists' Magazine* (Society of Genealogists, London), XXIV, pp. 1–4

# Index